# WINNING THE LIFE INSURANCE GAME

# WINNING THE LIFE INSURANCE GAME

## how you can get good protection and still save money*

by

J. J. BROWN

Author of *Start With $1000*

Macmillan of Canada
A DIVISION OF CANADA PUBLISHING CORPORATION
Toronto, Ontario, Canada

CANADIAN CATALOGUING IN PUBLICATION DATA

Brown, J. J. (John James), 1916-
Winning the life-insurance game

Bibliography: p.
Includes index.
ISBN 0-7715-9803-3

1. Insurance, Life. 2. Insurance, Life—Policies.
I. Title.

HG8773.B76 1985      368.3′2      C84-098977-6

Designed by: Leslie Smart and Associates

Macmillan of Canada
A Division of Canada Publishing Corporation
Toronto, Ontario, Canada

Printed in Canada

To the memory of my father, John Henry Brown, whose life in business epitomized the golden rule.

Three thousand years ago Confucius placed honest names at the top of the list of requirements for order and good government:

> The pupil Zilu told Confucius, "The Prince of Wei is proposing to entrust you with the government. What, in your view, should first be done?"
>
> The Master replied, "The most pressing need is to begin by correcting appellations. . . .
>
> "If appellations are incorrect, words fail to accord with reality. If words fail to accord with reality, the business of government cannot be carried on. If the business of government cannot be carried on, morality and harmony suffer. If morality and harmony suffer, penalties are wrongly imposed. If penalties are wrongly imposed, people don't know what to do with their hands and feet.
>
> "That is why the superior person considers it needful that appellations be correct, and that his words be correctly translated into action. He tolerates no disorder in his words."
>
> Confucius, *Analects*, translated by Wickert

# Contents

# Preface

*It has been very difficult to get published, in any newspaper of wide circulation, any searching criticism of life insurance companies.*
ELIZUR WRIGHT, 1847

Forty years ago I made the basic decision which in time made me a millionaire. This was the decision to "buy term insurance and invest the difference". I was then a poor university teacher still buried in debt, and if I had allowed myself to do as the insurance salesmen said, and had bought "cash value" or "permanent" insurance, I would never have had money to invest in the ventures that made me rich.

I have spent much of the past forty years trying different ways of convincing my fellow Canadians that they should buy life insurance my way. These have all been "rational" approaches, like this analysis of whole life or "permanent" insurance:

A conventional "level premium", "permanent" policy consists of some term insurance and some savings. Either you own your savings or you don't. There is debate about this in life insurance circles. If you (1) own your savings, the protection decreases each year. Thus the protection is not permanent. If you (2) do *not* own your savings, the protection remains the same, but each $1,000 is made up of, say, $980 insurance plus $20 savings. Thus, the insurance costs more each year. Therefore, if it were really "level premium", you would pay *less* for your protection each year. But it is not, so you pay the same.

No matter what the insurance company ads say, or what the nice salesman tells you about who owns the savings portion, it is impossible for any policy to have both permanent protection and a level premium.

There are plenty of examples in the book, larded with actual case histories, some going back the full forty years of my experience as a consultant. But basically I think this rational approach has failed. I

I

know that sales of term insurance to individuals used to be 7 percent of all individual sales, and that last year they reached nearly 27 percent (depending on whose figures you use), but this is caused by inflation, not by people reading my books.

I want to convince you that you should take my word for it that the life-insurance industry as a whole, and most of its individual salesmen, do *not* have your best interests at heart. If, after reading my story and learning something about the machinations of the life-insurance people, you come to trust me, good. Then I can tell you exactly what to do to get the best insurance protection for the least money, and, if you are already insured, how to turn in your garbage policies for ones that give real protection. The autobiographical bits will also warn you against hoping that newspapers, ombudsmen, consumer protection agencies, private and governmental, can or will help you get a fair deal from the life-insurance industry. They will not.

I have chosen the policy of using premium rates and examples covering the forty-year period 1943 to 1982 because:

1. It improves the chances of showing an example that is easily comparable with the reader's own policies.
2. It illustrates the changes in rates over forty years.
3. It allows the use of actual cases, whose history and final payout I know.

Since 1943, when I began my one-man campaign to reform life insurance, the industry has grown twelve times in annual premiums, sixty-four times in sales, twenty times in assets. More people own life insurance now than at any time in history, and life-insurance premiums still take up a large part of the average family budget.

Some of my more rational friends have ventured to ask: "Why not quit while you're behind? Why waste time bugging an established industry that is far out of your league?"

The answer, like the industry itself, is not simple. In 1970, when the arrogant U.S. automobile industry was pushing out ten million ill-designed, vulgar gas-guzzlers, fully equipped with built-in obsolescence and sleazy financing, it would have taken a bold man to say: "Two years from now, one of the four auto manufacturers will be effectively bankrupt, and sales will be down below six million units." But some of us did. Like the U.S. auto-makers, the life-insurance people have had a long run and have never considered the real needs of their consumers; management has become fat and torpid. The industry is still big, not to say monstrous, but in recent years there have been signs that it is not without some fierce internal stresses. The industry's share of the consumer's investment dollar has been dropping since 1965, yielding more and more to bank plans and mutual funds. The basic split in the industry between companies who still say a dollar is a dollar and those who have noticed inflation came into the open in the early sixties. Even with inflation down to an annual rate of 5 percent, this problem is not going to go away. As *Fortune* (July 14, 1980, p. 87) aptly says: "Inflation has left whole-life half dead." Those master money-managers, the life-insurance executives, had substantially all their assets tied up in low-yield investments at a time when interest rates soared and every other investor was making money.

But the low return on investment is only a small part of the story. All "whole life" contracts contain a clause permitting you to borrow the cash value at say 6 percent. This doesn't hurt the company when interest rates are 5 percent, but when they go to 20 percent, as they did in 1979, even the dumbest policyholder begins to ask himself: "Why am I paying 22 percent at the bank when I can borrow my own money for only 6 percent?" So the demand-loan depository aspect of the life-insurance business, which had been lying there ticking away like a time bomb for a hundred years, finally came into play. Wide use of the borrowing right, and mass cancellations, caused many companies serious liquidity problems in the spring of 1980. The next spasm of high interest rates could sink some of the weaker companies, and lobotomize the rest.

Finally, a declaration of my own interest. I keep up with the often shocking news of this industry as a public service, and write about it in the hope of making reforms and thus leaving the world a shade better than I found it. I have long since ceased to pay life-insurance premiums, having become self-insured some twenty years ago.

I must apologize for the soft and gentle diction used in this book in order to make it fit comfortably within the strict Canadian laws on defamation. I feel strongly about the harmful effect of this industry on society, but I cannot *speak* strongly. I had hoped that I would be able to quote earlier investigators, but I find that, under Canadian law, reviving someone else's defamation is just as actionable as

uttering your own. I had hoped that I could use some more outspoken words the same way they have been used for fifty years in
respectable publications in the United States, but I am told that U.S.
libel laws are much more permissive than ours. I had hoped that I
could use words that earlier Canadian writers on life insurance had
used—and got away with—in the past, but I was told that only fly-by-
night, small publishers could do this, because they were too small to
sue.

In spite of the difficulties above, and in spite of my own natural
inhibitions as a certified Canadian WASP, I trust I have made my
feelings about the life insurance industry amply clear.

J. J. Brown
1984

# PART I. Introduction

# Chapter 1 Your Choice

*To know, and not to do,*
*is not to know.*
YUKIO MISHIMA

When you die, your wife is going to pose a question to your executor. Because women are so practical, she is going to ask just one thing: "How much did he leave?" Among the questions she will *not* ask are:

—What kind of insurance did he carry?
—How much did he pay in premiums?
—Did he get good dividends on the policy?
—Was the agent who sold it to him a genuine Chartered Life Underwriter?

You cannot go far wrong in buying insurance if you remember that the main reason for having life insurance is to protect dependants, and whether you support your spouse or your spouse supports you, the breadwinner should be insured—and the more you give your heirs, the better they will like you after you have gone to your reward.

I believe that you are being swindled by the smoothest, most respectable con men in existence. How can you put an end to being a victim? There are only two ways: you can come to trust me and then do what I tell you, or you can learn the facts from this and other books, and then trust *yourself* for intelligent handling of your own affairs. The one person you must not trust is the insurance salesman. He is not "your" agent. He works for, is licensed by, and is under the complete control of his company. Neither should you trust a life-insurance company. Many of them have proven time after time that they are prepared to take advantage of the poor and ignorant. I go into this in more detail in later chapters, citing not merely my opinion, which might be the result of a casual snit against the industry, but the carefully considered words of chief justices of the U.S. Supreme Court, famous lawyers, millionaires, respected college professors, financial experts, and several presidents of life-insurance companies.

**What This Book Is About**

The premium you pay for life insurance covers the cost of two services—protection for your dependants if you die, and savings for yourself if you live. You pay for both these services, but unless you have mastered the trick of being alive and dead at the same time, you can't possibly receive both services. If you die, your heirs collect the death benefits, and if you live, you can collect part of your savings by cashing your policy and losing your protection; but in either case half of what you have paid for is never received.

This book explains the workings of a tested method of insuring and saving in separate programs, so that if you die, your heirs receive the death benefit and your savings, and if you live, you can enjoy your savings without giving up your insurance. To do this you *buy term insurance and invest the difference*.

This sounds very simple, and it is. But as usual there is a problem. The insurance companies have arranged through their flunkies in the various legislatures that you have to buy life insurance from their salesmen. This man is paid for his work by means of a commission on the premium you pay for the insurance. Since the more you pay the more he earns, you would be foolish to expect him to sell you low-cost protection. He will do it only after exhausting all his arguments for the high-cost types. The difficulty of the "buy term and invest the difference" plan lies in persuading the salesman to sell you the kind of insurance you need. To do this you have to study the examples that follow, and learn how to defeat the agent on his own ground.

Specifically, this book explains in simple terms how you can get more insurance protection for your money right now. It does not explain the Massachusetts system of savings-bank insurance, because not all of you live in Massachusetts; it does not tell you how fine everything would be if the government took over the sale of life insurance, because this has not yet taken place, and you are interested in saving money now. Books on all these subjects can be found in the Bibliography. This book does:

—explain how to get the greatest protection from each insurance dollar,
—tell you how to avoid—as far as is possible under the present system—being taken in by the life-insurance companies,
—name names, and make objective comparisons of policies offered by the different companies,

—explain the maneuvers the insurance agents will use to keep you from buying the best kind of insurance, and show you how to outmaneuver the salesman in his own field,

—provide graphs and tables that supply anyone between the ages of twenty and sixty-five with material to make out a personal life-insurance plan,

—show you how to calculate how much you are losing each year on your present policies,

—outline the simple steps required for changing your insurance over to the cheaper and better plan,

—discuss history, illustrating the criminal past and questionable present of the industry.

**Some Simple Examples**

Here is a simple question for anyone about to buy insurance. If you should die at twenty-five, leaving your spouse with the job of bringing up the children, which do you think she would rather have, $100,000 cash from Occidental Life, or $1,700 cash from Eaton Bay? The choice of insurance is entirely up to you. The same premium of $176 a year will buy either policy. Or, say you are forty. The need for insurance is not as great as it was when you were twenty-five, and, also, with a more senior job you can probably afford a larger annual premium. But for the sake of simplicity, let's ignore both of these factors. At age forty the choice is this: For an annual premium of $176, the death benefit can be either $53,000 from Occidental Life's term policy, or $2,000 from Eaton Bay's endowment-type policy. Surely this is not a difficult choice to make.

Or, say you married late, your spouse is fifty, and you have children still in school. For the same annual outlay of $176 you can have death protection of $22,000 from Occidental Life or the same $2,000 from Eaton Bay. The choice is up to you.

Looking at the question of "how much?" from the opposite side, you can see in Table 1 how much you have to pay at age twenty-five for each $1,000 of protection.

This range of prices for the same protection may make you wonder about the moral standards of the industry you have to deal with. An individual can be persuaded to pay two hundred times as much for his insurance protection as does a medical doctor in Ontario or the Maritimes. Does this seem fair to you? Medical doctors are late

| Company | Plan | Annual premium per $1,000 |
|---|---|---|
| New York Life (Ontario Medical Association) | RCNP[2] term* | $   .50 (net) |
| North American Life (Canadian Professional Engineers) | RCNP[2] term | .80 |
| Canadian General LIC (Ontario Pharmacists Association) | | 1.16 |
| Occidental Life | RCNP[2] term | 1.76 |
| Norwich Union | Life to age 65 | 15.17 |
| Crown Life | Whole life participating | 17.43 |
| Prudential of America | 20-pay life | 22.10 |
| Union du Canada | 20-year endowment | 44.33 |
| Standard Life | 10-year endowment | 52.90 |
| Eaton Bay | 10-year endowment | 103.10 |

*See pages 51-2 for an explanation of RCNP[2]. It's just a quick way of saying "the best".

**Table 1.** *Cost per year of $1,000 protection. Age 25. 1982 rates. Policy fees and underwriting fees not considered.*

starters in the earnings sweepstakes, but once they get going they are, on average, the highest-paid profession.

If your budget allows only so much money to spend on insurance each year (say $100), you can make up a table like Table 2.

## Death Benefit and Investment Value

These tables prove beyond argument that the more you pay for insurance, the less your heirs will receive when you die. Why, then, do most people buy the high-premium types of insurance? One good reason is that the salesmen make much more commission on the high-premium types; and salesmen, like the rest of us, have to live. Another reason is that people are so confused by life insurance that they think they can live and die at the same time, and so make a profit out of the insurance company.

| Company | Plan | Premium per $1,000 | Approximate death benefit |
|---------|------|---------|----------------|
| Occidental | 1-year renewable term | $ 1.87 | $53,475 |
| Metropolitan | Decreasing term (20 year) | 2.06 | 48,543 (1st yr.) |
| Eaton Bay | 5-year renewable term | 2.91 | 34,364 |
| Metropolitan† | 25-year mortgage term | 2.94 | 34,014 |
| Commercial | 10-year renewable term | 3.42 | 29,240 |
| Continental† | 20-year convertible term | 4.99 | 20,040 |
| North American* | Whole-life preferred | 5.75 | 17,391 |
| Occidental | Whole life | 13.54 | 7,380 |
| Mutual of Canada* | 20-pay life (non-smoker) | 19.89 | 5,027 |
| Confederation* | 20-pay life | 23.73 | 4,214 |
| Sun Life | 20-year endowment | 46.01 | 2,173 |
| Eaton Bay | 10 year endowment | 103.10 | 970 |

*Participating
†Convertible only
Policy fees ranging from $15 to $200 not considered

**Table 2.** *Amount of protection a premium of $100 a year will buy under the various plans. Age 30. Dividends not considered. 1982 rates.*

Let's take a careful look at the possibilities after you have signed your name to an insurance contract. First of all, you will either live or die. There are no other possibilities. Now, if you live, you will do one of two things: either you will keep paying premiums, or you will stop paying them and forfeit the policy. If you keep paying premiums, you are interested only in the death benefit, because the cash value is obtained only by relinquishing the policy. So in this case forget all about cash value. If, on the other hand, you give up your insurance and leave your family without protection, you are going to be interested in the cash value.

The second possibility is that you may die. If this happens, neither you nor your widow has any interest in the *cash value*, because the insurance company takes it all. The only thing your widow cares about is the *face value* of the policy—the death benefit. This is the amount the company pays your estate after subtracting any loans you have taken against the policy.

It is important to keep these two aspects of insurance well separated in your mind. The first, what money you can get out if you live, is the *investment value* of your plan; the second, the total amount paid your estate if you die, is called the *death benefit*.

If you live, the insurance plan with the highest investment value is best; but you might suddenly die, in which case the plan with the highest death benefit would be best. Since you can't tell which of these will happen to you, the idea is to work out an insurance plan which protects you in either eventuality. You want a plan which provides as large an investment value as possible, and at the same time provides a large death benefit.

Not only are there incredible differences in the price you can pay for the same service, but the life-insurance industry is the locus classicus of smug doubletalk. So you have to be careful, just to know what you are buying. In insurance, words mean what insurance salesmen have decided they will mean, just as in *Alice in Wonderland*. All the words used by company men to describe insurance policies have respectable, reassuring sounds. The most confidence-inspiring insurance name very often means just the opposite. For example, "absolutely safe" means subject to all the normal investment risks plus guaranteed lack of provision for inflation. In the life-insurance industry, "conservative" means *really* conservative. The actuaries boast of their use of conservative mortality figures, assume that 100 percent of their clients will die, and charge rates based on this figure. In actual practice the average mortality rate is only 54 percent. So nearly half the premium was charged needlessly. The big talking-point in the salesman's spiel and the company ads is "permanent" insurance. They say cash-value insurance is good because it is so "permanent". But look what happens in an actual policy. Here is a Prudential of England 20-pay life policy taken out in 1939 at age 36, for $10,000. (Though this policy is some forty years old, and thus allows an overview, if you were to make the same calculations using up-to-date rates the results would be essentially the same.) For the first two years the policy really is permanent, believe it or not. Had the owner died, his heirs really would have received $10,000. But beginning with the third year the policy suddenly acquires a cash value of $420. This climbs rapidly to $2,090 in the tenth year, and $5,030 in the twentieth year. Thus, instead of "permanent" protection, this policy actually gives protection of $10,000 for the first two years, $9,580 ($10,000–$420) in the third year, $7,910 ($10,000–$2,090) in the tenth year, and $4,970 ($10,000–$5,030) in the twentieth. Thereafter it declines continuously. Though the heirs would receive $10,000 if he died in the twentieth year, over half the death benefit is his own money! (If this sounds complicated, don't worry. I go into cash value in detail later on. See pages 91-2.) So, in life insurance, permanent means temporary.

Similarly, in the upside-down world of the life-insurance industry:

"Guaranteed" savings contrast with the fact that many policies end by lapse (see pp. 95, 99-101).

"Dividend" is something that is not the result of dividing profits.

"Level premium" plans all have steeply rising premiums per $1,000 of insurance protection (see p. 90).

In "20-pay life" you pay for twenty years—and then you keep on paying forever (see p. 92).

"Persistency" is the name given to the *lapse* rate.

"Cash value" is so called because it is *not* cash, it has no value to you, and you don't own it.

# Chapter 2 What Life Insurance Is

*The major problem in the life insurance market today is the lack of good solid reliable information at the point of sale concerning the benefits and prices of the insurance they are proposing to buy.*
    JOSEPH M. BELTH, ex-industry executive and Professor of Life Insurance, Indiana University, 1973

Before we can talk intelligently about an individual insurance plan, we must have a clear understanding of what life insurance is. In spite of the complications of most policies, life insurance itself is anything but complicated. It is a device for mitigating the financial effects of a common misfortune by spreading the loss over a large number of people. This is not a gamble but a scientific business worked out from vital statistics and the mathematical laws of probability.

Mortality tables (see Appendix 5) are available which show that of every 1,000 Canadian males beginning their thirtieth year, one will die in the next twelve-month period. The 1,000 men therefore agree to protect their dependants by paying $1,000 to the widow of the unidentified man who is to die. This means that each of the 1,000 men will have to pay $1 for his insurance protection that year. This is the cost of pure insurance.

There are two really great things about life insurance. You don't know about them because the salesman and his company don't *want* you to know. The first marvellous thing about it is that it is cheap. This means that everyone can afford it. When marketing, administrative, selling, and commission expenses are minimized through group policies, life insurance up to age forty costs next to nothing. The companies will go to any length of chicanery to keep you from learning this simple fact.

The second piece of good news about life insurance is, when it starts to get really expensive at age 65, you are normally too old to need very much. In the U.S. 1954 mortality table used for determining most premiums (see Belth, p. 252), only 8 percent of the mortality cost is from age 0 to 65, while the remaining 92% is from age 66 to 100. Look around you and use your common sense. How many of your neighbors have forty- to forty-five-year-old children who are dependent on them financially?

## Life Insurance and Fire Insurance

Pure insurance—without a savings component—is the rule in the fire-insurance business, but it is rare in life insurance. When you insure your house against fire, you pay $6 for each $1,000 worth of protection at the beginning of each year. You pay $6 and not $10 because in the district where you live approximately 6 houses out of every 1,000 are damaged by fire each year. If at the end of the year your house has not burned down, you lose your $6. In other words, you pay your money for service, the protection for your home for one year. Once this service has been rendered, there is no reason why you should get your money back.

The reason the insurance companies do not try to sell 20-pay fire-insurance policies is that most fire policies are bought by business men, who (when they are not blinded by sentimental considerations) feel that it is foolish to pay for anything in advance. Most life-insurance policies, on the other hand, are bought by people with little business experience, and, moreover, by people who do their buying in a sentimental haze.

If the fire-insurance companies operated like the life companies, your fire-insurance policy would be something like this: Instead of $6 per thousand you would pay $10. Of this amount, $6 would be put aside by the company to pay the claims for the following year, and the rest would be called the "investment value". After you had paid $10 a year for several years your insurance policy would begin to have a "cash value", because the overpayments of $4 a year had been accumulating at interest. After a while you would have the privilege of borrowing up to 96 percent of this cash value and paying interest on it at the rate of 6 percent.

But if you should happen to have a fire after borrowing your own money, the company would not pay the full amount of the claim, but only the difference between the face value of the policy and the money you had borrowed. Say your cash value had built up to $1,000, and after you had borrowed $800 at 6 percent your house burned down. Instead of paying the face value of the policy ($1,000), the company would pay only $200—because, they would say, they had already paid you $800.

So it appears that as soon as the cash value of your fire-insurance policy approaches the face value, you are really insuring *yourself.* And then you begin to wonder: since you are insuring yourself, and will pay any losses out of your own pocket anyway, why keep on paying premiums to the insurance company? But the company has an answer to that one. They say they are willing to give you the cash value if you surrender the policy, but if you do this your insurance in the future is going to cost you much more. If you take your cash value and start again, the insurance will cost $16 a thousand, because with the passage of years the house has dried out considerably and is not a good fire risk.

If this 20-pay fire-insurance policy sounds like a good buy to you, my advice is that you stay out of business, because your talents obviously lie in a different field. The conventional life-insurance policy is, if anything, a worse investment than the 20-pay fire-insurance policy, because you always need protection against fire, but when your dependants leave home you no longer need life insurance.

### The Increasing Cost of Insurance with Advancing Age

Since men are more likely to die the older they become, the cost of insurance must increase with advancing age. This is a statistical fact, and no amount of juggling with figures, no new insurance plan explained by a friendly and persuasive salesman, can get around it. The usual method of sugar-coating this bitter pill is to double or triple the insurance premiums early in life in order to build up a surplus which will take care of the increased cost of insurance in later life. But you are not likely to need insurance in later life, so why pay for it when you are young?

In any case, the amount of overpayment in early life is much larger than it needs to be. One reason for this is that the rates are made up on the assumption that a man aged 95 (the terminal age varies from one insurance company to another) still needs to be insured to protect his children in case of his untimely death. The fact that the children have by this time reached the ripe age of 65 and are themselves ready for retirement does not seem to have occurred to the insurance companies.

A second circumstance that makes money for the companies is the undeniable fact that money earns interest. In determining how much overpayment should be made early in life, the companies conveniently forget to mention this fact. A $20-a-year overpayment earning interest at 12 percent, compounded annually, grows to $8,620 at the end of thirty-five years.

## The Many Names and What They Hide

The simple fact is, there is only one kind of *insurance*, namely term insurance. But the other fact is that nothing is allowed to be simple in the life-insurance industry. People might begin to understand what they are buying. I have made a list of over two hundred different names for life-insurance policies, ranging from ordinary life to the latest idiot's-special policy, where you *borrow* all the money required to pay the premium. All these policies are achieved by adding different amounts and types of savings schemes to the basic chicken stock of term insurance. Sometimes the cook, desperate for something new, will add spices, such as deferred premium payments or automatic borrowing.

## Prepayment

Premiums must increase as you grow older, for the simple reason that you are more likely to die. Since people hate to see their premiums getting larger every year and might drop the insurance when the premiums get unbearable, the companies hide the increase this way: they take all the premiums you would pay until age 95 and divide this by the number of years you have to pay. This gives a level premium, which you pay until the policy is paid up. At age 45 you pay perhaps $39 a thousand instead of, say, $18. This is bad for you and good for the insurance company for two reasons. First, you may not want insurance at age 95, either because you have died, or because your children have all grown up and can take care of themselves. Second, as I have mentioned, the difference between $39 and $18 begins to earn interest as soon as you pay it to the insurance company, but in most cases it earns interest for the company, not for you. Why not keep it working for you? The rate at which money grows is shown in Appendix 3.

Even quite immature minds can understand this with regard to common things they buy, but almost nobody is able to figure it out when it comes wrapped up with an insurance policy. When I was doing some hangar flying at the airport, two high-school boys came in to see about learning to fly. The manager explained to them that they could either pay for the lessons one at a time as they took them, or deposit a lump sum in the office and draw against it as the lessons progressed. They saw at once that the first plan was better because their money could keep earning interest for them in the bank until it was needed, instead of earning interest for the flying school.

## The Kinds of Insurance

In spite of the number of different policies the agent displays, there are really only two kinds of life insurance. In the actuarial textbooks these are called prepaid, and pay-as-you-go. In a sense all policies are prepaid, because you must pay for insurance in advance. But the difference in the two types is in the number of years you pay in advance.

When you buy prepaid insurance (ordinary life, endowment at age 65 or 85, family income, 20-pay life, 20-year endowment, and so on), you pay for protection thirty or more years in advance. If you buy a policy for an unborn child, you can prepay as much as ninety-five years! When you buy pay-as-you-go insurance (1-, 5-, 10-, or 20-year term), you pay for your protection 1, 5, 10, or 20 years in advance. By paying premiums monthly, you cut down the prepayment time as much as possible; but companies charge extra for monthly or quarterly payments.

Insurance salesmen do not like to use the word "prepaid", because it makes some people think they are paying for something long before they need it. This is exactly what they are doing. To avoid this unpleasantness the companies use the word "endowment", or the phrase "paid up at age 65". Such words and phrases give the buyer a comfortable feeling, but the facts remain unchanged. These facts are that money earns interest, and the money you pay out in advance for life insurance might just as well be earning interest for you as for the company.

*Comparing prepaid and pay-as-you-go (term) insurance cost*

| | Gross premiums per $1,000 | | | | |
| | Age 20 | Age 30 | Age 40 | Age 50 | Age 60 |
| --- | --- | --- | --- | --- | --- |
| Prepaid (ordinary life) | $14 | $19 | $27 | $40 | $68 |
| Prepaid (20-year endowment) | 47 | 51 | 54 | 61 | 80 |
| Pay-as-you-go (one-year term) | 2 | 3 | 4 | 8 | 19 |

**Table 3.** *Comparative cost of policies*

Most insurance companies push only prepaid types of insurance; the wise buyer of insurance should be willing to consider only the pay-as-you-go types. A glance at Tables 3 and 4 will show why.

**Flexibility**

Prepaid policies can be changed only at great financial loss, and since the company already has your money in its coffers, you are not in a very strong bargaining position to force a change that is favorable to you.

Pay-as-you-go policies can be changed easily, simply by cancelling one policy and taking out another. Since the company knows very well that you can do this, it will often give you a good deal on a conversion.

**Eventualities**

When you take out any insurance policy there are four things that may happen: you may die, you may find you no longer need insurance and cancel the policy, you may want to borrow on the policy, or you may find yourself unable to pay the premiums. Let's look at each of these possibilities in turn.

(a) You die

If you have paid for insurance in advance up to age 95, you are bound to lose money if you die before that time. With any prepaid policy you lose money if you die before the terminal age.

With any combination of ages and duration of policy the results are always the same. Prepaid insurance always turns out to cost from three to eight times as much as pay-as-you-go insurance, for the same

*Example 1*
*Policy taken out for $1,000 at age 20, policyholder died at age 30.*

|  | Ordinary life | 20-pay life | 10-year term |
|---|---|---|---|
| Total premiums paid over the 10-year period (neglecting interest) | $156 | $263 | $50 |

*Example 2*
*Policy taken out at age 30, policyholder died at age 50.*

|  | Ordinary life | 20-pay life | 10-year term |
|---|---|---|---|
| Total premiums paid | $383 | $584 | $144 |

**Table 4.** *Loss through death before terminal age*

death benefit. We are ignoring the so-called cash value of all policies, because we are talking about the first eventuality: death. When your policy terminates by death, the cash value disappears.

(b) You cancel

The second possibility is that you cancel the policy. When you do this with a prepaid policy you lose your shirt. Short-term cancellations, of course, are the most damaging, but with all prepaid policies you lose if you hang onto your policy and you lose if you cancel it. The only thing you can do, in this case, is to lose as little as possible.

(c) You take a loan on the policy

The third possibility is that you run short of money and want to borrow on your policy. When you do this, the company keeps charging you for the full amount of the policy (you keep right on paying premiums) and in addition gets 6 percent on *your* overpayments, which have been lent back to you temporarily. Moreover, your dependants are left with only partial protection, since you have really

*Metropolitan Policies for $10,000—Age 30*

|  |  | Endowment (20-year) | Ordinary life | 10-year term |
|---|---|---|---|---|
|  | Amount of premiums paid, with 4% interest | $ 6,080 | $2,840 | $1,140 |
| Policy surrendered after 10 years | Cash value plus dividends | 4,658 | 1,736 | 410 |
|  | Net cost | 1,422 | 1,104 | 730 |
|  | Amount of premiums paid, with 4% interest | 15,000 | 7,020 | 3,335 |
| Policy surrendered after 20 years | Cash value plus dividends | 11,722 | 4,271 | 620 |
|  | Net cost | 3,278 | 2,749 | 2,715 |

**Table 5.** *True net cost of various types of policy*

borrowed money from them. You don't need a table to figure this one out.

(d) You go bankrupt

The last possibility is that you reach a point where you can no longer pay the premiums. If the 30 days' grace elapses and you have not acted to get your cash-surrender value, the automatic-borrowing feature of your policy comes into force. By this means the company will borrow *your* money to pay *its* bill, keeping you insured by "extended-term insurance" until the cash value of your policy has been exhausted.

## The Kinds of Prepaid Insurance (arranged in order of decreasing cost)

This section is inserted chiefly for reference so that you can turn to it quickly when the salesman comes up with an alleged new kind of policy. On a first reading, just skip through the section lightly. If your own policy goes by any of the names below, watch out.

## 1. 10-year endowment

This combines the features of a limited-term policy with the investment hazards of a beginner playing the stock market. You pay so much a year for ten years, and at the end of this period your insurance contract comes to an end and the company pays a cash sum sometimes as much as 60 percent of the total amount you have paid in. This puts all the odds against the buyer.

## 2. 20-year endowment

This is a great favorite, because both salesman and company make a wonderful profit from it. Just like a 10-year endowment, except that the payments are spread over 20 years.

## 3. Miscellaneous endowments

They can be had for terms of 5, 15, 25, 30, and 35 years from some companies; but no matter how long they last they are bad for you. The rule is: never buy an endowment. The longer the endowment period, the worse it is for you. The reasons are obvious if you stop to think about it. The effect of compound interest is greater in later years; and, since the older you are, the closer to death you are, you have less chance of enjoying the money from the endowment.

## 4. 20-pay life

You make 20 equal payments spread over 20 years, and then the insurance is "paid up" for the rest of your life. This too is bad for you. Never touch it.

## 5. Miscellaneous x-pay life policies

This type may be had with the payments spread over periods of 5, 10, 15, 20, 25, 30, and 35 years, but no matter how short a time you pay, you lose every time. Never buy x-pay life.

## 6. Endowment at age 65, 70, 75, 80, etc.

This is a variation of the endowment scheme, the number of payments depending on your age. Everything said about 10- and 20-year endowments applies. Never buy one to mature at an early age. Those which mature at age 85 are simply ordinary life policies.

### 7. Whole life paid up at age 65, 85, etc.

This is like 20-pay life except that the cash payments end at a definite age. Never buy it for maturity at an early age. If it matures at age 85 or 95, it is simply an ordinary life policy.

### 8. Ordinary life

This is the commonest policy. You keep paying premiums each year until you die. This can be useful under certain special circumstances, but the ordinary buyer shouldn't touch it.

### 9. Special types of ordinary life

Some companies issue special $5,000 whole-life policies, or a "banner" or "anniversary" series, which in some cases cost you less than the ordinary life policies. But make a careful mathematical analysis before buying.

### 10. Double-protection policy

This is an ordinary life policy to which have been added a few drops of term insurance to make it smell sweeter. You pay a premium every year until you die, but if you die before a certain age the death benefit is more than it is after that age. Not a good buy.

### 11. Family-income policy

This is a form of double-protection policy in which the death benefit (if you die within 20 years) is paid to your wife in the form of so much a month for a certain number of years. Not usually a good buy.

### 12. Deferred participation

All the so-called participating policies are deferred, since they do not begin paying dividends until the third year (for a further discussion of dividends, see p. 102). But some companies issue an extra-deferred-participation policy which begins paying dividends only after the fifteenth year. Avoid it.

### 13. Level-premium term

The cost of term insurance is averaged over a number of years between your age and age 65, and this is the premium you pay. Avoid this, because you are paying too far in advance.

### 14. Retirement-income policies

These are also called life income, annuity, pension plan, combined assurance, pension policies, and so on. They are a mixture of life insurance and a deferred annuity in one policy. Never touch one, even with a long pole. If you live, you have no insurance protection, and if you die, the company keeps your savings. By assuming a sufficiently low interest rate—3 percent or less—it can be shown that the insured's savings portion is gradually returned to him when the life insurance expires and the retirement income begins, if he is long-lived. But, of course, everybody (except the insurance company) earns more than 3 percent on savings today.

### 15. "Buy term and invest the difference" policies

The life companies, after denigrating and sneering at this principle for generations, have now adopted it as the latest stroke of genius of the industry. You can now buy policies which do all the work for you: the company takes your money, buys term insurance with part of it, and invests the remainder in short-term investments at reasonably high interest rates. Some policies guarantee 4 percent on the investment portion, but give you credit for more if the earnings turn out to be higher.

As usual, the names given these policies do not describe what they really are. It would not do to mention term insurance.

### 16. Universal life

Introduced by E. F. Hutton Life in 1980, this has caught on, and is now the stock in trade of several small companies such as Transport Life, Jefferson National Life, Liberty Corporation, and other groups no one has ever heard of. You will notice that the big, well-established companies like Equitable and Prudential do not have it. Insurance executives call it "Cannibal Life", because its sale results from twisting. That is, policyholders will buy universal life and then turn in their old cash-value policies, which have been rendered farcical by inflation.

Compared to standard cash-value policies, universal life has much to recommend it. The death benefit is adjustable, as is the annual premium. In good times you can get reasonable returns on your savings portion, and you can borrow (under some fairly strict conditions) on your accumulated cash value. But why not go all the way and do what I recommend? Separate your insurance and your savings. Then you can buy the cheapest term insurance, and at any given time enjoy the best return on your savings.

If you don't want the bother of looking after your savings, there are plenty of people around who will do it for you. You don't have to trust your money to a life-insurance company. The banks now are all offering RRSP (Canada) and IRA (United States) plans where you get some tax deferment on the income; and mutual funds are available to put you into almost every type of investment there is. And now, with lots of competition, you can get the convenience and management of mutual funds without having to pay through the nose.

### 17. Adjustable life

This is universal life with one of the benefits removed. The death benefit and the premium can be changed, but the return on investment is fixed.

### 18. Variable life

This is universal life with something different removed. The return on the savings may turn out to be high in good times, but you can't change the premium. The death benefit depends on the eventual return on equity investments.

### 19. Complete life

Another universal life put out by an E. F. Hutton subsidiary in California, E. F. Hutton Life.

### 20. Cost-of-living insurance

This is a name used for policies whose death benefits follow the rise in the cost of living. You are allowed, at a price, to increase the face value 15 percent or $30,000 a year (whichever is the lower), without having to take another medical examination.

But the cost of doing this is ridiculously high to begin with. Sun Life of America, for example, offers $100,000 of original coverage under its "Checkmate" plan (well named), for $1,504 a year at age 35. Occidental Life will sell you the basic $100,000 of protection for $230. That is, for one-sixth the money, you can get the same basic coverage without the hoopla.

| Company | Plan | Yearly Premium* at | | | |
|---------|------|------------|---------|---------|---------|
|         |      | Age 20 | Age 30 | Age 40 | Age 50 |
| Standard Life | 10-year endowment | $1,047 | $1,048 | $1,058 | $1,082 |
| Excelsior Life | 10-pay life | 406 | 487 | 606 | 768 |
| New York Life | 20-pay life | 234 | 288 | 365 | 480 |
| Metropolitan Life | Whole life to 65 | 153 | 216 | 332 | 601 |
| Sun Life | Ordinary life | 138 | 184 | 259 | 386 |
| Mutual Life | Special-rate life | 142 | 189 | 266 | 399 |
| Manufacturers Life | Level-premium term | 55 | 73 | 107 | 164 |

*to nearest dollar. 1963 rates. Participating

**Table 6.** *The yearly cost of $10,000 of insurance under various prepaid plans*

John Hancock Mutual has the same policy on offer in its Flex-Five plan, at a premium of $587; Mutual of New York will sell you their CPI Life for a premium of $2,220.

These "new" policies are the work of a desperately mismanaged industry, trying to sell more insurance at high prices.

## Tax Status

In addition to ridiculous pricing, there is another disadvantage to all universal-life policies. The IRS has given a "private letter" ruling allowing deferment of taxes on the cash value of universal-life policies until the owner cashes in (as in an RRSP). But Massachusetts Mutual Life (and all the big companies with a vested interest in the status quo) is fighting this ruling, saying that the difference between the 4 percent guaranteed and the actual interest is really a dividend. The big companies may win, and force the IRS to reverse itself. In any case, the exact tax status of this type of policy is not clear, and probably will not be clear for some time.

# PART II. How To Do It Yourself

# Chapter 3 How To Arm Yourself with the Needed Skills

*Our study of this industry dis-*
*closes that American consumers*
*are losing billions of dollars yearly*
*as a result of ill-informed and*
*inappropriate life insurance pur-*
*chase decisions.*
FEDERAL TRADE
COMMISSION, 1980

Recently the life companies have been bragging that it costs them over $100,000 and $10,000 in overhead to train a salesman. What they want you to believe is that you are getting some high-priced help at no cost. What I want you to believe is that the life companies are serious about wanting to take your money from you in the traditional way. This means that *you* must be serious if you want to hang on to your own money.

Being serious means making a careful study of the two skills you must have before you can win at the life-insurance game. These are:

1. Learn some simple mathematics and how to read a graph, so that you can put a mass of facts into a simple and understandable form; and

2. Learn the arguments that the salesman is going to use on you, so that you can see them coming and refute them with ease.

### Making and Reading Graphs

The type of picture best suited to demonstrating facts that have to do with numbers is called a graph. Graphs are pictures, and pictures help you to see at a glance. Take for example a simple natural phenomenon that everyone has noticed: the fact that it gets hotter in the middle of the day, and colder at morning and night. The meteorologist at the weather bureau puts this information in the form of long lists of numbers which look something like this:

| | A.M. | | | | | | P.M. | | | | | |
|---|---|---|---|---|---|---|---|---|---|---|---|---|
| Time | 2 | 4 | 6 | 8 | 10 | 12 | 2 | 4 | 6 | 8 | 10 | 12 |
| Temp. | 35° | 45° | 50° | 60° | 70° | 75° | 80° | 75° | 70° | 60° | 50° | 40° |

But it is simpler to make a picture or graph. So we mark off a sheet of paper in equal squares and say that the horizontal lines represent temperature, the vertical lines time. If we begin in the lower left-hand corner, time will pass as we move horizontally to the right, and the temperature will increase as we move upward. This squared sheet with its labelled lines is called a graph.

Now take a pencil and transfer the information in the table to the grid. First we see that at 2 A.M. the temperature was 35°, so we make a dot at the point where the line representing 2 A.M. crosses that representing 35°. Do the same for all the pairs of numbers in the table, and join the dots with a curved line. Then you have a graph something like the one in Figure 1.

By glancing at the picture you can see immediately what kind of day it has been. If the graph in Figure 1 is considered to show a

**Figure 1**  Temperature Graph of a Normal Summer Day

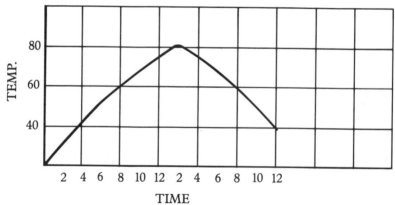

**Figure 2** Temperature Graph of a Queer Day

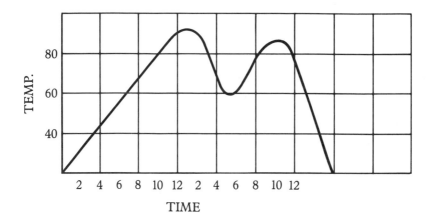

normal summer day, when a graph like the one in Figure 2 appears, you know at once that the day has been very unusual.

A graph, then, is simply a picture of a set of figures. It lets you know the trend of the figures without getting bogged down in the details.

**The curves which tell you how to make your life-insurance plan**

Pictures of insurance needs, insurance policies, and savings plans are just as easy to make as those of the weather, and what they reveal is much more important. To make a graph of your insurance needs, let the distance across the horizontal line be time in years, and the distance up the vertical line the total amount of insurance needed in dollars.

The life-insurance needs of the average married man are not constant, but look something like those depicted in Figure 3. He starts out with no insurance, because he has no dependants, but when he gets married at age 20 he buys insurance to protect his wife. In his thirties, when he is carrying protection for both his wife and his children, the line reaches its highest point. But in his forties the children start to leave home and the amount of insurance protection he carries begins to drop. By the time he is 50 all the children have gone. The insurance drops still more, and since his wife dies when he is 60, he is able to drop all his policies, being back where he started forty years before, with no dependants.

**Figure 3**   Graph of Life-Insurance Needs

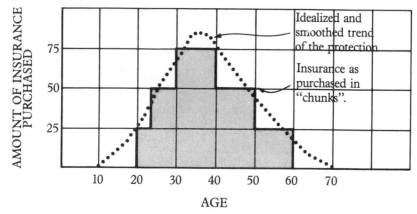

The general shape of this curve is the same as a child's drawing of a mountain. It begins and ends at the bottom of the page and rises fairly sharply in the middle. Of course, your particular insurance needs may turn out to make a flat-top mountain when drawn, or the sides may be less steep, but the general shape of the curve will be as shown.

Now, any space under the line is going to cost you money, because it represents the insurance on which you are paying premiums. The height of the mountain represents the sum of your insurance, and the thickness of the mountain tells you how long you have to keep paying premiums. If your insurance needs look like those shown in Figure 4, you are a lucky man, because the mountain is not very thick, and you will not have to pay heavy premiums for very long.

If, on the other hand, your graph looks like the one in Figure 5, you are going to be in bad shape financially, because the mountain is very thick and the period of heavy premiums lasts a long time.

### Making a graph of an insurance policy

Once you know your insurance needs, and have pictured them in a graph, the obvious thing to do is to make corresponding graphs of the various types of insurance policies to see which one is best suited to your needs. All your graphs are drawn on the same type of graph paper and have the same numbers and units along the edges. This is

**Figure 4** Narrow Mountain

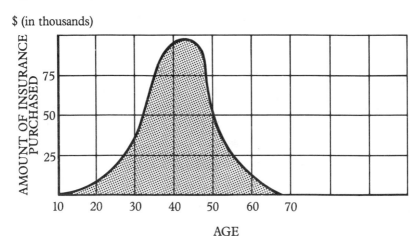

so that two mountains which are the same height on the two graphs represent the same amount of money, and two cliffs which appear at the same point on two different graphs are showing sudden changes at exactly the same time.

Now, if you could get an insurance policy whose graph was exactly the same as the graph of your insurance needs, it would be ideal. But

**Figure 5** Wide Mountain

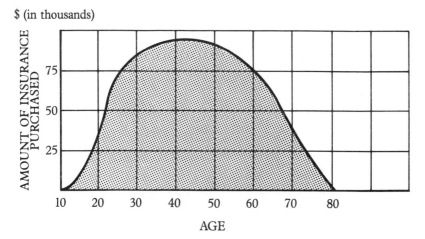

**Figure 6**   Graph of Ordinary Life

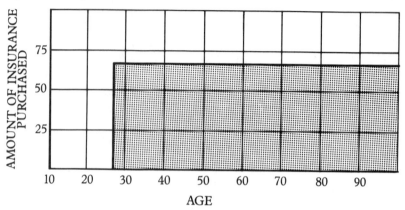

$ (in thousands)

in this world below, such things seldom happen. Let's try one common type of policy to see how it looks—the old standby, an ordinary life policy. Its graph is shown in Figure 6.

All prepayment types of insurance (see pp. 22-5) have graphs that look like the one in Figure 6. True, you can take out several policies at different times, and thus get a graph looking like the one in Figure 7.

**Figure 7**   Graph of Ordinary Life: Staggered Beginnings

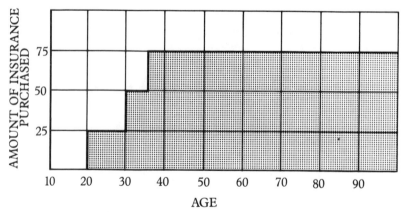

$ (in thousands)

Remember that you have to pay for everything underneath the line, so when the line goes straight off the right side of the page at the $75,000 level, you are going to remain poor. With all policies that have graphs like these, the so-called "permanent" insurance, you must pay for having insurance at age 90 or thereabouts, whether you need it or not. Some people don't need it because they are dead. The rest don't need it because they have no dependants. What we require to fit the graph of our insurance needs is something more flexible.

Look at the graph shown in Figure 8 for 5-year term renewable to age 65.

**Figure 8**   Graph of 5-Year Renewable Term

$ (in thousands)

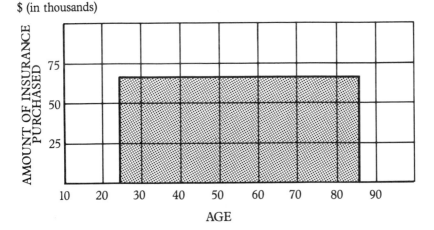

You can see at once that this is getting closer to what we need. It is possible to take out policies at different times, as before, to get a graph which looks like the one in Figure 9. In addition we can cancel the policies at different times to get a graph like the one shown in Figure 10.

This would seem to be the ideal type of policy for our purpose, because we can get almost any shape of mountain by varying the times at which we buy and cancel the various term policies. But there is one difficulty. All kinds of insurance get more expensive as you grow older, but term gets extremely expensive, because you have not been paying for it in advance. After age 55 it gets too expensive for

**Figure 9**   Graph of 5-Year Renewable Term: Staggered Beginnings

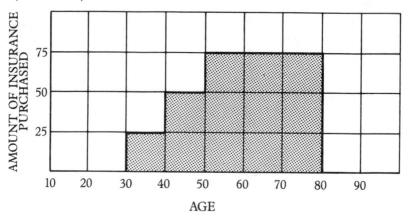

**Figure 10**   Graph of 5-Year Renewable Term: Staggered Beginnings and
                Ends

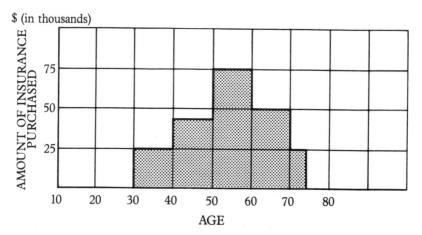

ordinary use (nearly $20 a thousand), and will have to be dropped.
On dropping all term insurance at age 55, we get a graph like the one
in Figure 11.

This is the one we are going to use in our insurance plan. It gives
us a left-hand side that can be adjusted to any degree of steepness to

**Figure 11** Graph of 10-Year Renewable Term Dropped at Age 55

$ (in thousands)

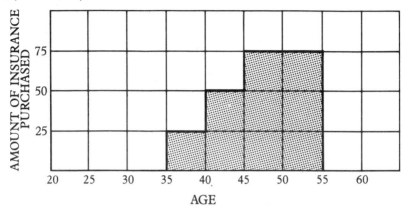

fit our graph of insurance needs; but the right-hand side is a cliff, and will not do. The way we adjust this is by means of your own separate investment plan. The most conservative investment possible is a bank 5-year savings certificate, which I use as an illustration. There are many other possibilities.

### Making a graph of a savings plan

This is done with the help of the tables in Appendix 3, or by using your desk calculator. Look up the column headed "Amount of 1 per period" on the 12 percent sheet (this percent is used simply as an example; when doing your own, use current rates). At the point where the "5 years" line and the "1 per period" file meet, you find the figure 6.352. This means that $1,000 a year for five years deposited into a savings account will amount (neglecting taxes) to $6,352. Mark this point on your graph, five years out vertically, and at the $ level indicated. Do the same for 10, 20, and 30 years, using the figures given in the table. Join the dots and you have the required graph. Its general shape will be like the one in Figure 12.

Note that the general shape of this curve is that of a mountain that is high at the right-hand side. The general shape of the term-insurance graph is that of a mountain that is low at the right-hand side. Put them both together and they spell security (see Fig. 13).

**Figure 12**    Graph of Savings Plan

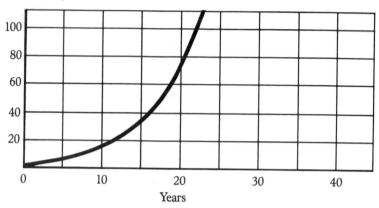

The term insurance holds up the left-hand side of the graph, and when it begins to get expensive around age 55 you drop it. Then the insurance value of your savings plan takes over and holds up the right-hand side of the graph until you die.

Now compare the graph of the term-savings plan with the graph

**Figure 13**    Combined Graph of Insurance and Savings

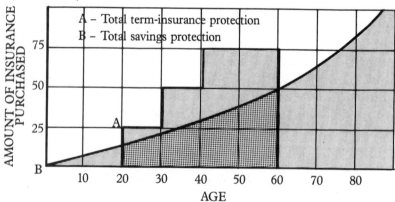

we made of your insurance needs. It is clear at once that they are the same general shape, and any small changes required to make them fit exactly can be made by changing the savings plan, or the time at which the term insurance is dropped. Now we have a general picture of a plan which will protect our dependants if we die, and ourselves if we live, all at the smallest possible cost.

# Chapter 4 Choosing the Best Term Insurance For You

*You can't buy insurance at these prices anyway.*
HARVEY ENCHIN,
Montreal *Gazette*, 1982

Now that you know enough to buy nothing but term insurance, you think you are home free. But no. There are dozens of kinds of term insurance, and you must know how to choose the one that is cheapest and best fits your needs. Besides, banks, department stores, trust companies, and others not historically in the insurance business are beginning to get serious about selling term insurance. So for the first time in history there is some competition.

**How Much Should You Pay?**

This sounds simple but it is not. Life-insurance companies have a two-hundred-year history of hiding their prices, and a well-worked-out system of avoiding direct comparability between policies. So the simple advice "buy the cheapest and forget it" will not work.

Actually, the price question can best be approached in two stages. First, you get the price down from $12 a thousand to $2 a thousand. This is done by choosing term insurance rather than any type of cash-value policy. Second, you try to fine-tune the price down from $1.90 to $.35 a thousand.

But low premiums alone are not enough. There are other key factors that must be considered in a policy, such as:

—are renewal rates guaranteed or not?
—can you renew without medical examination to age 65 or age 80?
—is the insuring company large, solid, and stable?

These and other factors are changing all the time. For example, New York Life has come out with a policy that sells for $1.13 a thousand at age 30. This is cheap, but there are some quirks in the renewability conditions.

What matters is not what the salesman *says*, but what is written in the contract itself or at least in a printed brochure. With a document, you at least have a case in court. If a company won't let you have a sample contract, forget it. Some contracts don't specify renewal rates. Forget them.

Remember that death rates are falling, hence the cost of life insurance should keep on falling. Prices that look low today should seem outrageous in another ten years.

Perhaps the best general advice I can give is to use the services of a life-insurance broker, and pay him for his work. Let him collect the best rates for you, read the actual policies, and make sure they contain no jokers that a layman like you might miss. Most brokers are operating now in the province of Quebec, and also to a lesser degree in Alberta and British Columbia, but I think they will be coming to other provinces fairly soon. All sorts and conditions of people are eligible for low group-insurance rates. For example, American Express card-holders, members of a union such as the Teamsters, and people who put their money in certain banks can all get special low rates. A good insurance broker will know of the opportunities in your community, and will tell you where to buy.

## The Types of Term Insurance (in approximate order of increasing cost)

### 1. Decreasing face-value term

This is also called declining, or reducing, or "mortgage" term. The premium remains the same each year, but the amount of protection declines each year as you get older. The amount of coverage can decline in several ways: either a fixed reduction each year, or five years with no reduction and then the beginning of decline, or a decline that is tied in with the year your children leave school. This is still the cheapest and perhaps the best kind of insurance for wage-earners. It gives maximum protection for the least money when your children are babies, and the need to replace your wages would be acute.

But decreasing term is subject to the serious objection that, in times of inflation, the coverage decreases just when you want it to *increase.* I happen to think that inflation is going to continue for the foreseeable future at at least a 5 percent rate, with excursions from time to time back up to the 15 percent annual rate. But I may well be wrong.

## 2. Group term for professionals

Look into this type first. It may give you all the coverage you need—cheap.

If you are a medical doctor, nurse, lawyer, accountant, teacher, engineer, or pharmacist, check first the group rate for your age with your professional association. New York Life makes money selling insurance to their friends the doctors at 50 cents a thousand at age 30. The company's term rate for individuals at that age is $2.80 a thousand. Doctors get shot by disturbed patients, cut during operations, exposed to nameless germs, bacteria, and rare Oriental diseases. They also have a high rate of early death from hypertension, and they smoke a lot, asking for lung cancer. Nevertheless, judging from the low rates, they are the favorite risks of New York Life. So by all means take advantage of any low rate offered to members of your profession. The limit is usually $300,000 coverage, which is plenty.

## 3. "Death" mortgage insurance

This is a new type of term insurance made available by most Canadian mortgage lenders, such as banks and trust companies. It is difficult to compare prices, because the insurance is "free". That is, the premium is hidden in the monthly interest and principal payment on the mortgage. But the coverage is cheap, and insurance companies hate it. If you have, or are about to have, a mortgage on your home, you should look into this type of life insurance.

## 4. Convertible term

This is issued in periods of 5, 10, 15, and 20 years, but at the end of the period you cannot renew the policy. You must convert it to one of the higher-premium prepaid types. Never buy it.

## 5. Limited term

Another name for convertible term. Issued to cover periods of 5, 10, 15, and 20 years. The policy does not say so, but the fact is that these contracts cannot be renewed without medical examination. Do not touch it.

## 6. Renewable term

Some companies give this name to their limited-term policies, so be careful when buying it. Make sure that the policy states clearly that it can be renewed without medical examination. This type of policy can be obtained to cover periods of 1, 5, 10, 15, and 20 years, and can be renewed without medical examination any time before your 85th birthday. Whether you buy for the 1-, 5-, or 10-year period is a matter of convenience and personal preference. The longer periods are not recommended, since they are less flexible.

## 7. Group insurance

This is a term policy which is subject to various conditions. You must work for a given company, and usually the amount of insurance you are allowed is determined by the size of your salary. For example, university teaching staffs are allowed $25,000 worth of group insurance for a salary under $30,000, $40,000 if it is under $50,000, and so on. Of course when you leave the employ of the company you lose the term-insurance protection. Your only recourse is to convert to higher-premium types.

Some companies insist that you join their plan as a condition of employment. Most companies not only get you a group rate that is much cheaper, but also pay part of the premium for you. The Montreal *Gazette*, for example, pays half the group premium, so younger staff people there get their life insurance for 48 cents per $1,000 of protection. These are the same people who let one of their staff writers say that it is impossible to buy life insurance at $1.70 a thousand. They don't even read their own paychecks.

## 8. Savings-bank term

If you live in the right state (Massachusetts, New York, Connecticut) and don't require a lot of protection, this might be a good buy. You buy it over the counter at the bank, and you don't have the traumatic experience of fighting the salesman. At the bank, he gets paid whether or not you buy. This is still not available in Canada.

## 9. Mail-order term

Respectable merchants, such as Sears and Eaton Bay, sell term insurance by mail. This protection is often cheap, because there is no commission for the salesman, and there are no high agency costs. All you have to pay for is the insurance, and this is cheap.

Before signing a mail-order policy application, get a report from your local Better Business Bureau about the company. This can be done by phone. Sears Roebuck is certainly all right, and so is Eaton Bay, but get a second opinion on any mail-order company whose name is not familiar.

## 10. Swiss "death risk" insurance

There is no law (yet) that says you have to buy your life insurance in an unstable currency. The Swiss franc, over the past fifteen years, has been 400 percent stronger and more stable than the U.S. dollar, and 500 percent stronger than the Canadian. Had you bought a Swiss life-insurance policy fifteen years ago and died last month, your wife would now be paid off in 100-cent instead of 20-cent dollars. This is worth thinking about. The Swiss companies will accept your payment of premiums in Swiss francs, and will make a contract with you to pay off in Swiss francs. This currency will have its own fluctuations, but nothing like the hair-raising ups and downs of the dollar.

For information, write to a company, specifying "death risk" insurance, and giving age, occupation, and state of health. The Swiss consulate in Ottawa, Vancouver, Montreal, or Toronto will give you other addresses, but here is one: Swiss Life Insurance Company, 40 Quai General Guisan, 8022 Zürich, Switzerland. They speak English.

| Company | Plan | Yearly premium* at | | | |
| | | Age 20 | Age 25 | Age 35 | Age 45 |
| --- | --- | --- | --- | --- | --- |
| Dominion Life | 5-year term | $200 | $200 | $260 | $569 |
| Eaton Bay | 5-year term | 190 | 262 | 323 | 589 |
| Occidental Life | 6-year term (N.S.)† | 115 | 115 | 142 | 283 |
| Occidental Life | 1-year term | 156 | 161 | 230 | 480 |
| La Sauvegarde | 5-year term | 199 | 199 | 230 | 502 |

*1980 rates (Male)
†N.S.—Non-smoker
Policy fees ignored.

**Table 7.** *The yearly cost of $100,000 insurance under various pay-as-you-go (term) plans*

## Making Your Choice

In choosing the term-insurance policy best suited to your needs, you have a choice in three areas:

—face value: fixed or decreasing each year
—participation: participating or non-participating
—length of period: 1, 5, or 10 years, or to age 65.

## Decreasing Term or Fixed-Face-Value Term

Decreasing term is the cheapest way of protecting a family. If you have a little money and a large family, some sort of decreasing term plan is probably your best bet. Under this plan, at age 25 you can buy $100,000 worth of insurance at an annual cost of $160. The face value of the policy decreases each year, but the premium you pay remains the same. Thus, if you are lucky enough to die during the first year, your family gets $100,000 and you have paid only $160. If you die during the fifth year the death benefit is only $80,000 instead of $100,000, and at the tenth year the death benefit is only $57,000. After twenty years the insurance coverage drops to zero. Thus the insurance costs you $1.60 a thousand when you are poor and struggling under the burdens of a large family, and $5 a thousand ten years later when presumably things are better.

Normal contract periods are 15, 20, 25, and 30 years, but most companies do not allow expiry dates that come after age 75. It is possible to get any contract period that suits your needs (for example, 21 years) at corresponding rates.

The policy may be converted to fixed-face value at any time at your option. Say that after five years of the policy used as an example above you have a sickness that prevents your ever passing a medical examination again. At this time you could convert your $80,000 term policy into an ordinary life policy with a face value of $80,000. This you could do as a matter of right, without medical examination, and it would assure you of $80,000 of insurance for life. But of course the premium would be considerably higher than that of the decreasing term policy.

## Rates for Decreasing Term

As is usual in the life-insurance industry, decreasing term is usually called something else. The names usually given to this type of policy are good-public-relations terms like "family provider", "income protection", or "family security". What you want is not the family-security rider sold by most companies, to be attached to a cash-value policy to make it smell better, but the family-security policy, which stands by itself. Another problem is the comparison of rates for this type of policy. All companies selling it quote the rate per $10 of monthly income, as shown in Table 8.

| Age at issue | Occidental | Metropolitan* | Dominion |
|---|---|---|---|
| 20 | $1.98 | $ 3.88 | $ 3.54 |
| 25 | 2.08 | 4.23 | 3.67 |
| 30 | 2.24 | 5.08 | 4.07 |
| 35 | 2.79 | 6.87 | 5.25 |
| 40 | 3.99 | 10.15 | 7.36 |
| 45 | 6.16 | 15.41 | 10.97 |

*Participating policies.
1983 rates.

**Table 8.** *Rates for income-protection policies (per $10 of monthly income)*

But what you really want to know about any policy is how much each $1,000 of protection is costing you each year. Since the face value of a decreasing-term policy decreases each year, the protection increases in cost each year. Here is the calculation you have to make to determine your actual cost:
Example:

At age 40, 20-year decreasing term costs, say, $3.99 for $10 a month.

At a 3 percent rate the commuted value of an income of $10 a month for 20 years is $1,814 (see Table of Commuted Values, Appendix 6). Since in the first year of the policy's life the company would have to pay either $10 a month for 20 years or the equivalent commuted value (the owner of the policy has the right to choose which), your actual protection this year is $1,814. This is costing you $3.99. So, to get your rate per $1,000 of insurance, divide $3.99 by $1,814 and multiply by 1,000, giving a rate of $2.20.

At the end of the fifth year the amount of cash required to pay $10 a month has dropped to $1,456, since the payments have to be made for only 15 years instead of 20. This sum, divided into $3.99 and multiplied by 1,000 as before, gives you the rate of $2.74 per $1,000.

Making the same calculations for the later policy years, we get rates as follows:

10th year: $3.84 per $1,000 of insurance
15th year: $7.15 per $1,000 of insurance

The income period on this type of policy can be anything from 10 to 35 years. Table 9 shows actual rates being paid per $1,000 of protection on policies started at various ages, for two different contract periods.

*Rates per $1,000 annually at issue*

|         | Contract Period | |
|---------|---------|---------|
| Age     | 15-year | 20-year |
| 20      | $ 1.60  | $ 1.64  |
| 25      | 1.66    | 1.69    |
| 30      | 1.83    | 1.85    |
| 35      | 2.43    | 2.49    |
| 40      | 3.49    | 3.67    |
| 45      | 5.53    | 5.71    |
| 50      | 8.44    | 9.01    |
| 55      | 12.42   | 13.92   |
| 60      | 18.36   |         |

**Table 9.** *Decreasing term insurance. 1983 rates, Occidental Life.*

Any decreasing term policy should be dropped when it has only five more years to run. Because of the comparatively small amount of insurance remaining in force, the rate per $1,000 ceases to be advantageous.

From these tables you can calculate the premium you have to pay for a policy with a given starting face value. (The longer the life of the policy, the more you pay per year.) From Tables 9 and 10 you can

|                                      | Contract Period |         |         |         |
|                                      | 15-year | 20-year | 25-year | 30-year |
| --- | --- | --- | --- | --- |
| At issue                             | 100%    | 100%    | 100%    | 100%    |
| After 5 years, protection remaining is | 72    | 80      | 85      | 90      |
| After 10 years, protection remaining is | 38   | 57      | 69      | 76      |
| After 15 years, protection remaining is | 0    | 30      | 48      | 60      |
| After 20 years, protection remaining is |      | 0       | 26      | 43      |
| After 25 years, protection remaining is |      |         | 0       | 23      |
| After 30 years, protection remaining is |      |         |         | 0       |

**Table 10.** *Rate at which the protection decreases*

easily calculate how much insurance you will have in force at any time during the life of the policy. For example, say at age 30 you choose a 20-year term and a policy with a beginning face value of $50,000. Your premium each year for 20 years would be $92.50 (50 × $1.85). After 15 years, when you are 45, the face value of the policy will have dropped to $15,000 (30 percent of $50,000).

Fixed-face-value term is very simple. If you buy a policy with a $50,000 face value, it keeps that face value for its entire life. If you buy a large amount (say $300,000), it is sometimes cheaper per thousand than decreasing term.

### Participating or Non-Participating?

In my earlier books on life insurance (written in the early forties and early sixties) I came out moderately in favor of participating policies. In these, the company makes an overcharge in the premium, and, if all goes well, they give some of it back to you in later years. There is often a large differential between the overcharge on a term policy and the overcharge on an endowment, yet the so-called "dividend" goes at the same percentage rate to all policyholders. This means that term-insurance owners get a larger slice of the pie than do the suckers who bought endowments. Now, even if this remains true, I have ceased to recommend participating term policies. The main reasons for this are:

1. You lose control of your own money for a period of years. During this time you can invest it much better than an insurance company.

2. Dividends are not guaranteed, and may be stopped, at the company's whim, at any time. Moreover, there are now studies of insurance company dividends, going back many years, which contrast the anticipated dividends (which persuaded people to buy) with the actual dividends paid. Those paid are usually much less, which is to say that the policies are bought because of false expectations. My friend Frank McIntosh put out one of the earliest studies of this type (see Bibliography).

3. Dividend has a dictionary meaning. It means a share of the net profits of an enterprise after all expenses have been met. What the industry calls a "dividend" is simply the eventual return of a gratuitous overcharge in the premium. The way to prove to anyone that it is not a "dividend" is that the fisc has never attempted to tax it.

4. The fact of inflation means that you should enjoy the use of your own money now, not give it to an insurance company at zero interest. You not only lose control of your money, as I mention in number one, but inflation causes you to lose control of its purchasing power.

## Comparing Prices

By now you know enough never to buy anything but renewable term insurance; the only question is, which company sells the cheapest? So you shop around to get the best bargain in renewable term. In Appendix 4 you will find tables comparing the term policies sold by the various companies. Table 11 shows a simplified table for age 30.

In 1944 the replies to a questionnaire that I sent to all Canadian life companies indicated that only 11 of the 95 companies licensed to sell insurance in Canada sold pure insurance (without a savings component). Of these 11, very few were big-name companies who advertise in the daily papers. Metropolitan was an outstanding exception, and most of us know New York Life, but who has ever heard of Paul Revere, United Benefit, or Maritime Life? The big advertisers, the big spenders of their policyholders' money, were hiding coyly in the wings when it came to selling pure insurance.

| Company | 1-year | 5-year | 10-year | Per $10 mo. income | To age 65 | Decreasing (20 year) |
|---|---|---|---|---|---|---|
| Dominion Life | $2.00 | $2.08 | $ | $ | $5.01 | $1.36 |
| Manulife | 2.06 | 2.65 | | | 5.39 | |
| Eaton Bay† | 1.32 | 2.97 | 3.08 | 4.07 | 3.27 | |
| Metropolitan* | | 3.74 | | 5.08 | | 2.06 |
| Occidental | 1.74 | 2.10 | 2.49 | 2.24 | 4.51 | 1.85 |
| Paul Revere | | 2.37 | | | 5.57 | 1.93 |
| Fidelity‡ | | 1.88 | | | | |
| Equitable | 1.90 | | | | 5.30 | |
| Cumis Life* | 2.53 | 2.88 | 3.32‡ | | 6.09 | 1.98 |
| Prudential of America* | 2.91 | | 3.34 | | | 2.47 |

*Participating
†Non-smoker
‡Convertible but not renewable
The premiums given are for $1,000 worth of insurance at age 30.
Note that six of the companies do not pay dividends (i.e., are non-participating). 1980 rates.

**Table 11.** *Prices of various kinds of renewable term insurance*

In 1963, when I made a second survey of the industry by question-naire, the line-up of companies had changed somewhat, but only 6 sent me complete rates. It is still next to impossible to find out from reference books such as Stone & Cox whether a given company sells term insurance that fulfils our basic conditions: being renewable and convertible in the same face amount without medical examination.

You will notice that only four of the companies listed in the simplified table pay dividends on term policies. The Metropolitan has a fairly high dividend rate, and is one of the strongest companies financially. But we must remember that dividends are not guaranteed, and may be stopped at any time.

### The Choice among Non-Participating Term Policies

From Appendix 4 it is apparent that the same term protection can be bought for various prices. There is no difficulty about comparing policies that run for the same length of time; but if you want to compare, say, 10-year renewable with yearly renewable, you must look to the past. Table 12 shows two actual policies going back forty years.

| | Premium per $1,000 | |
| Year | Mutual | Occidental |
|---|---|---|
| 1st | $ 7.11 | $ 8.31 |
| 2nd | 7.16 | 8.31 |
| 3rd | 7.22 | 8.31 |
| 4th | 7.28 | 8.31 |
| 5th | 7.34 | 8.31 |
| 6th | 7.39 | 8.31 |
| 7th | 7.44 | 8.31 |
| 8th | 7.48 | 8.31 |
| 9th | 7.53 | 8.31 |
| 10th | 7.58 | 8.31 |
| Average per year for 10 years | 7.35 | 8.31 |
| Average for 20 years | 8.30 | 8.98 |
| Average for 30 years | 13.35 | 11.20 |
| Average for 40 years | 24.50 | 18.71 |

**Table 12.** *Cost comparison at age 25 of Mutual yearly renewable term with Occidental 10-year renewable term. 1943 rates to permit 1983 comparison of actual policies.*

From this table you can see that the Occidental term is substantially cheaper if you keep it more than 20 years. The Mutual policy is slightly cheaper for the first 10 years.

However, as a new buyer there is no way you can get this perspective, so you should buy the cheapest one- or five-year renewable-term policy that fulfils *all* of the following RCNP[2] conditions.

1. *Renewable* without medical examination

2. *Convertible* to prepaid type without medical examination at age 65

3. *Non-participating*

4. *Pure*. No cash value, or saving component

5. *Permanent* to age 80 or higher

As an aide-mémoire, this is expressed in the letters RCNP[2].

It is also a good idea to make sure the company is known and recommended by the Better Business Bureau in your town.

## A Final Word

Banker's Life of Des Moines advertises in *Fortune:* "Yes, you really *can* get cash value life insurance at the price of term." In a way, it's true. Also, you can buy a Rolls-Royce for the price of a Lada. I know, because I have done it just recently. But, in *real* life, neither transaction is in the cards. The insurance company is peddling its "Adjustable Life" policy, which has a cost-of-living option that allows you to increase the protection every three years to partly offset inflation. But when you look up Banker's Life in the Consumers' Union Report on Life Insurance you find that it is not at the top in terms of low price (number 35 and 59 on the list of participating whole-life policies) and its best 29-year yield is only 5.41 percent compared with 7.64 percent for Teacher's (the leader).

The simple facts are these: if you take the most expensive term policy and one of the cheaper whole-life policies, and then wait thirty years, you may come out better with the whole life. But my argument is: 1. Why not come out better right now instead of having to wait thirty years? and 2. Always buy the cheapest term.

# Chapter 5 Making Graphs of Your Insurance Needs

*As a snow-drift is formed where there is a lull in the wind, so, one would say, where there is a lull of truth an institution springs up.*
  H. D. THOREAU
  Cape Cod

In Chapter 3 we worked out a general graph of the insurance needs of a married man. The curve had the general shape of a mountain, rising to a maximum height when the children were all dependent and then falling off rapidly as the children left home. Now we want to get down to cases and make a graph of your particular insurance needs. The general shape of all the graphs will be the same, but some will rise or fall more sharply than others, and the changes will take place at different times. (The single parent of either sex has exactly the same problem. You have people dependent on you, so you have to provide for their welfare after you are dead. If you are a female single parent you should buy insurance from a company smart enough to know that women live longer than men, hence should pay *less* for life insurance. Occidental Life has noticed this, and will sell you term insurance at the rate for men that is three years less than your actual age. They will also give you lower rates if you are a non-smoker.)

Your first step is to take a piece of blank graph paper and on it mark the points in your life when you expect interesting things to happen. Unless you are an expert with the crystal ball, this planning will seem difficult; but do the best you can, and don't worry too much about accuracy. Remember that the plan is flexible, and your holdings can be adapted quickly to suit changed conditions.

Most graph paper is divided by vertical lines into divisions, running across the sheet. Let each of the major divisions represent ten years, and mark your present age and this year's date on the line at the

53

extreme left. Then mark the age and date ten years from now on the next major division, and so on across the page.

Now draw a graph of your insurance needs on this sheet. (See Figure 14.) There are eight major vertical divisions on the graph paper, separated by horizontal lines. Start at the bottom, and allowing $100,000 for each large division, mark the amounts opposite each line up the left-hand side of the sheet. Now, before you are married you carry no insurance, because insurance is a device to protect dependants, and you have none. To indicate the fact that you carry no

**Figure 14**   Basic Graph

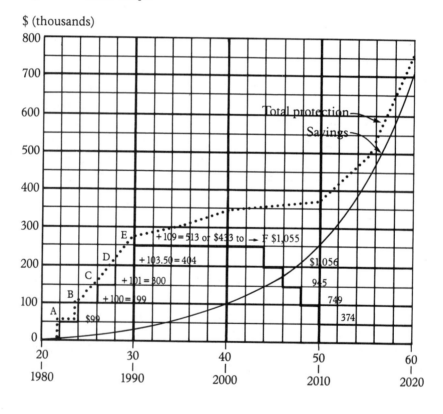

insurance in 1980, make a mark at the point where the 1980 line intersects the line which means zero dollars. Let us say you plan to marry in 1982. To protect your wife you will need, say, $50,000 worth of insurance. Therefore, at the intersection of the 1982 and $50,000 lines make a mark. This mark is labeled A on the graph.

When your first child arrives, say in 1984, you need more insurance, so you add another $50,000 policy, and mark a point B at the intersection of the 1984 line and that representing your total insurance, $100,000. Do this for all members of your projected family, say a child every two years until you have four, and you will end up with a series of points from A to E.

Now when your first child is 20 years old, it is reasonable to think he will no longer be dependent. So count over 20 years from his birthday, and on that line drop your insurance from $250,000 to $200,000 (F). Do the same for all the children as they cease to be dependent. You end up carrying only $50,000 worth of insurance in 2010, to protect your wife. Join these points by straight horizontal and vertical lines, and you have a graph of your projected insurance needs.

You will probably find, with your income, that you can't afford to buy all the protection you want. But the graph you have just drawn is useful nevertheless, because it shows the general trend of your needs. You will not have enough money to make the graph of your insurance holdings rise to the same level as that of your needs, but you can adjust your policies so that the contours of the two graphs are the same. The two graphs in Figure 15 show that this person is carrying less protection than he needs, but, because the two lines are roughly parallel, that he is doing the best he can on his income, and is carrying his maximum protection at the time he needs it most.

## An Alternative Method of Figuring Insurance Needs

The weakness of the method just described is that the sum of $50,000 for each dependant is an arbitrary figure chosen without much relation to the individual's income and prospects. An alternative method, which is more involved but more accurate, is to work from the life expectancy. First you find, from the life-expectancy table at the right-hand side of Appendix 5, how long you are likely to live. Then you figure the minimum amount of money that could maintain your family for one year. This amount will decrease as the children

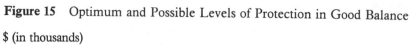

**Figure 15**   Optimum and Possible Levels of Protection in Good Balance

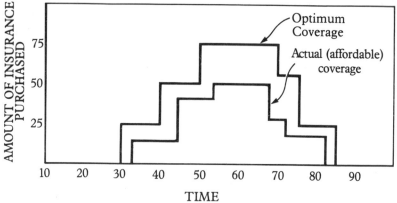

become independent, so you will have to take an average. Then, from the present-worth tables in Appendix 3, you find the present value of the amount of money needed to maintain your family, paid each year, for the number of years in your life expectancy, using a percentage that seems reasonable (say 10 percent). This will turn out to be a much larger sum than you can afford, so take one-quarter to one-half of it as the amount of insurance you need.

For example, say you are now 40 years old. Your life expectancy, from Appendix 5, is 33 years. Then say you decide that your family could survive on $10,000 a year. The present value of $10,000 a year for 33 years (from the table of present worth of one per period 10 percent, Appendix 3, Col. 6) is $95,694. This is the amount of insurance you should carry to give your dependents $10,000 a year. You may not be able to afford this because it costs $316 a year, so the next-best thing is to take as much of it as you can afford as the amount of insurance you should carry.

This method, too, has its disadvantages, because that's the way life is. Nothing is perfect, nothing free. One disadvantage of this method is that it makes no allowance for the fact that you keep getting older each year, and your life expectancy decreases. As it decreases, the present value of the sum required becomes less, so if you are paying premiums on an amount you calculated last year, you are paying too much. In practice you buy a little less than you need, and then over a 5-year period the average comes out right. Every five years you review your insurance needs, and make corrections as required.

## Another Alternative Method

Another way to calculate the amount of insurance you should carry is to make an estimate of your net money value as a wage earner. The first question is to determine your probable maximum salary, and how soon you will reach it. Then, from Appendix 3 find out how much these future earnings are worth today (Present Value of 1). Take, say, a 10 percent rate for the number of years of your life expectancy. This gross income must be diminished by the amount of money it costs to feed and house you, which you must estimate as best you can. Find the present value of these cost-of-living figures, and you get something like this:

Say you are 40. Then your life expectancy is 33 years.

Present value of gross annual future
earnings of $25,000 at 10% over 33 years is
25,000 × 9.569                                        $239,225

Present value of your future
costs of living (say $15,000
a year) at 10% is
15,000 × 9.569                                        $143,535

Net value of the individual at age 40                 $ 95,690

## Designing a Protection Plan to Cover Your Needs

You have now made, by one method or another, a graph or picture of your insurance needs. The next step is to design a plan to fit these needs. To do this you:

1. Determine how much you can set aside for protection.
2. Divide this between the insurance and the savings portions of your personal plan.
3. Make a graph of the term insurance that the insurance premium will buy.
4. Make a graph of the savings plan the balance of your money will buy.

5. Add the two graphs to get the complete picture of your protection plan.

## How Much to Pay?

The factors which tell you how much of your income you can afford to pay for protection are these:

### Size of your income

The more you earn, the more luxuries you can afford. Security is a luxury. Except in unusual circumstances, your bank savings, insurance premiums, savings-plan payments, and stock and bond purchases in any one year should not be greater than 10 percent if your gross income is under $15,000; 15 percent if it is between $16,000 and $40,000; and 20 percent if it is over $40,000.

### Number of dependants

The more people you have depending on you for support, the higher the percentage of your income you must spend for protection.

### Your nature

If you and your wife are healthy, risk-taking individuals, you will carry less insurance than if you are both timid types. If it is a mixed marriage of the type "he bold as a lion, she soft as a dove" (or vice versa), the amount of protection will have to be negotiated.

### Professional qualifications of your spouse

Obviously if your spouse is the self-reliant type you can spend a larger proportion of your earnings on current fun and less on protection. If you have married a computer programmer who was earning a living before you met, it is not necessary to carry much insurance. But if your partner has never worked and has no training in a profession, more protection will be needed.

### The age and nature of your children

The more children you have, the more protection you must carry. Also, the younger the children, the more they need to be protected by adequate insurance and savings. The nature of the children is very important in determining how much protection they need. If they are full of initiative, brilliant and enterprising, so there is never a dull moment at home, you can carry relatively less protection; they can take care of themselves. But if, on the other hand, your children are dull and torpid, sitting around the house waiting for someone else to make suggestions, then you must carry more insurance for them.

### Your life expectancy and profession

Do you come from a long-lived family? Are your father and mother still living, and did your grandparents on both sides of the family live to a ripe old age? If the answer to these questions is yes, you can afford to get along with less insurance. Remember that if you do not die, the insurance company wins, and you don't want that to happen. If you come of a long-lived family and, in addition, belong to a profession in which you can earn well after sixty, then your need for protection of all kinds is slight. Doctors and lawyers, for instance, often earn more after sixty than before. If other factors are right, they can afford to get along with very little protection.

After considering all the factors above, you are ready to make an estimate of how much you can afford for security. Say you are 20; you got married in 1980, have two children, and plan to have at least two more. You are now earning $20,000 a year and expect to reach a maximum of $60,000 about fifteen years from now. You plan to stay with your present company, and will retire on a pension at age 60. You plan to support your children for at least twenty years. Your wife has never earned her own living, and you are a rather conservative type. With this information you can make a good guess at how much of your present income you should spend for security. Say you decide to spend 10 percent. This means that you will have $2,000 a year for security plans. This is all shown in Figure 14.

### Dividing the Amount into Insurance and Investment

Many of the factors which you considered when you were trying to decide on the figure of $2,000 a year for all kinds of protection plans have to be looked at again when you determine how this sum is to be divided among insurance and various types of savings. To make it easier, let's start with a definite figure. As the result of my work on this subject I have come to the conclusion that the best normal division for an income at the $15,000 to $50,000 level is 80/20. That is, the money you save is spent 80 percent for savings and investment, and 20 percent for insurance. In your case, you have a total of $2,000 to spend; this means $1,600 for investment and $400 for insurance.

The conservative investment money each year might be divided something like this:

| | |
|---|---:|
| Liquid savings in a bank or easily cashed bonds | $  500 |
| R.R.S.P. | 600 |
| Securities portfolio | 500 |
| | $1,600 |

The insurance money should go to buy one-year or five-year renewable term insurance which fills all the requirements of RCNP[2]. One-year term is more easily changed as new children appear. Five-year term is less trouble. Both are cheap.

Some of the factors which will raise the proportion of life insurance to 30 percent or higher are these:

### Your health

If you are in good health now, but the chances of your health remaining good for ten or fifteen years are poor, then you may find it wise to take out more insurance than you need right now in order to be covered in the future. One way to do this is to choose decreasing term instead of one-year term. Say, for example, your father's side of the family has a history of some serious disease. It has not struck you yet, but genes being as they are, the chances are it will. You need only $50,000 worth of insurance to protect your family now, but within ten years you will need more. Any policy you buy now will be renewed without medical examination at the end of each year, but if your health is bad by that time you will not be able to get any more. In such a case it might be wise to buy $400,000 worth of insurance now, in complete anticipation of future needs.

### Your occupation

If you work at certain types of jobs, it is sometimes wise to over-insure temporarily in order to be sure of having the right amount of insurance when you need it. For instance, if you write books on life insurance which are critical of the companies, you would be wise to have all the term insurance you are ever going to need before the books are published. If you work at a safe desk job now, but think that eventually you will be sent abroad, you might have to consider taking out too much insurance. People who work abroad and admit it sometimes have trouble getting term insurance. Remember that neither the salesman nor the company wants you to buy term protection. This means they will seize on anything abnormal in your situation as an excuse for not selling it to you.

### Your prospective earnings

If you expect a raise soon, and you want to be certain of all the term insurance you need until you are 85, you might consider paying out a higher proportion of your $2,000 for insurance. The reason for this is that the insurance is the least flexible element of the protection plan. You can always drop it, but bad health or a dangerous occupation may keep you from increasing it. The savings plan, on the other hand, is eminently adaptable. You can either increase it or decrease it at will. Therefore, if you expect a substantially larger income, you might be wise to put more of your money into term insurance and less into the savings. Then when you get your raise you can make up the savings by the payment of a lump sum.

In the absence of any special reason for needing more insurance right now, try to keep the amount you spend on your insurance premiums at 20 percent of the total amount of money you put aside for security each year. This does not sound like much, and when you compare the amount you now have for insurance premiums with the amount you have been paying to the companies under your old plans, you will be astonished. But remember that your savings have an insurance value as well as the investment value, and therefore when you combine term insurance and savings your protection is adequate.

Now take out your graph (Fig. 14) again, and figure out how much the insurance is going to cost. The first policy, for $50,000, taken out to protect your wife when you were 22, cost $99; those to protect the children will cost $100, $101, $104, and $109. Add these figures to your graph, so you can see how much your protection is costing you at any time.

Life insurance prices are characterized by notching; that is, if you buy a lot, you can get lower prices per thousand. It pays to watch the notch, where the price drops because of volume. In the case of the policy used here, let us say that when you buy $250,000 of protection, the price (at age 30) drops to $1.67 a thousand. This means you can take out a new policy to replace all the others, at a cost of $433, and save $80 a year.

## Making the Graph of Your Savings Plan

The savings portion of your plan can consist of a fixed-dollar-value fund such as an annuity or a savings certificate or a variable-purchasing-power plan such as a mutual fund. For the illustrations that follow, I use the savings certificate simply because the figures are relatively certain. When you invest in equities the value of your fund can go up or down, depending on your fortunes in the market. But with a certificate the dollar value of the fund can only go up if you continue to make agreed payments.

This is not to say that the savings certificate is the best type of savings plan for you. Under today's circumstances it probably is not. If you invest sensibly in equities as a hedge against inflation, and if inflation continues, you will do much better than if you had bought savings certificates. Instead of earning 6 percent compounded annually, your savings portion might grow at the rate of 8 percent, 10 percent, or even 20 percent compounded annually. Neglecting the few hundred dollars a year you save in the first ten years because the insurance is cheap, you have now to draw your graph showing how the annual savings of $1,600 mount up at interest. I have chosen the rate of 10 percent compounded annually, since trust companies are now offering 11 percent for a five-year period. This gives a curve as in Figure 14. If you take a higher rate or compound more often than once a year, the curve will be steeper and more money will be available at any time. If you choose a lower rate of interest, or interest rates fall after five years, the curve will be flatter and you will have less money available.

Here is how to make the savings curve on your graph. Look up Appendix 3 and find the column "Amount of 1 per Period" on the page marked 10 percent. Opposite these years you will find these numbers:

| Year | Factor | times amount of savings, $1,600 = | Total |
|------|--------|-----------------------------------|-------|
| 5th | 6.105 | | $ 9,768. |
| 10th | 15.937 | | 25,499. |
| 15th | 31.772 | | 50,835. |
| 20th | 57.274 | | 91,638. |
| 25th | 98.347 | | 157,355. |
| 30th | 164.494 | | 263,190. |

| 35th | 271.024 | 433,638. |
|------|---------|----------|
| 40th | 442.592 | 708,147. |

Transfer the totals to the graph as before, and draw in the curve.

## Making the Composite Graph of Your Protection Plan

Now you have two pictures, one showing the amount of term insurance you are carrying at any time, and the other showing the insurance value of your savings program. In order to find out how much protection you are carrying, say at age 43, you add the two kinds of insurance you have. From the term-insurance graph, you see that the line representing age 43 meets the graph of your term insurance at the line for $250,000. So you have $250,000 worth of term insurance at this time. From the savings graph, you find that the rising line of the savings total crosses the age 43 line at approximately $140,000. Your total protection, then, at this time, is $390,000.

Take your term-insurance graph and your savings graph and make a table showing how much insurance you have each year you make a major change in the amount. The table will look something like the one in Table 13.

Now you have the figures needed to make the composite graph of your protection plan. Take your sheet of graph paper with the outline

| Age | Amount of insurance from term graph | Amount of protection from savings graph | Total amount of protection |
|-----|-------------------------------------|-----------------------------------------|----------------------------|
| 25 | $100 | $ 10 | $110 |
| 30 | 250 | 25 | 275 |
| 35 | 250 | 51 | 301 |
| 40 | 250 | 92 | 342 |
| 45 | 200 | 157 | 357 |
| 50 | 100 | 263 | 363 |
| 55 | 50 | 434 | 484 |
| 60 | 50 | 708 | 758 |

**Table 13.** *Total amount of protection at various ages, in thousands*

of your term-insurance graph and the outline of the savings amount. Now mark on the graph the points representing column 4 of Table 13. That is, make a dot at the intersection of $110,000 and age 25, $275,000 and age 30, $301,000 and age 35, and so on. Now use a different-color pencil to trace out the composite graph. Notice that the line is either vertical or roughly parallel to that of the savings. From this dotted line you can find out immediately how much insurance you are carrying at any time. The height of the line indicates the total amount of money that would be paid to your widow from all sources if you should die.

### Making Any Required Changes in the Composite Graph

If the graph looks all right for the first five years, leave it alone. In five years you will want to review your insurance holdings anyway, in the light of what has happened to your family and financial circumstances in the meantime. From your graph you can see that at the end of five years you will be carrying nearly $110,000 worth of insurance. This is made up of $100,000 worth of term and nearly $10,000 in the insurance value of your savings. If this is more than you need, simply delay taking out the third block of term insurance. The shape of the graph can be changed at will simply by taking out the blocks of term insurance earlier or later in life.

Figure 14 is the graph of a normal, well-insured person with a good savings plan. It is also the graph of a person in good health, with normal prospects of staying that way. Figure 16 is the sort of graph that appears when the wage-earner has a health problem, and decides to buy all his insurance needs at once. This approach is more costly, but a well-paid executive (who has other worries) might think it worth the money.

The plan is quite expensive because the one-year term insurance (the horizontal line at the $250,000 level) costs $380 the first year, $392 the fifth year, and $458 the tenth year. One way around this is to buy linear declining face-value term instead of one-year renewable term. This gives you a level premium of $380 a year. Its graph is shown in the dotted line beginning at the $250,000 level. Notice that this line is more or less the reciprocal of the graph showing the growth of the savings plan. This means that in any given year the *total* of the insurance and the savings plan will be about $250,000.

**Figure 16** Basic Graph for Someone with a Health Problem

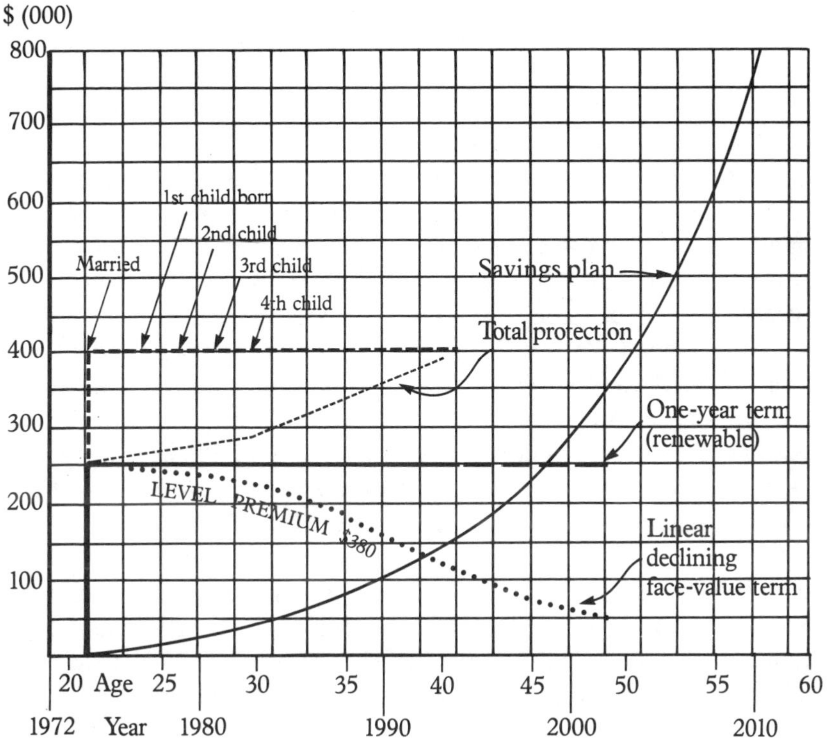

$ (000)

**Parameters:**

| | |
|---|---|
| Age 30 in 1983 | Retire at 60 |
| Started work 1972 | Insurance prem. max. $600 |
| Married 1974 | Total savings p.a. $2400 @10% |
| 2 children born 1977 & 1979 | 1 p.a. becomes 442.5 in 40 yrs. |
| 2 children to come 1981 & 1983 | Insurance costs $1.52 per. M. |
| Earning $30,000 | Buys $250,000, prem. $380 |

## How to Maintain and Service Your Protection Plan

One great advantage of the term savings plan is its adaptability to changing conditions. Under the best of circumstances life is a gamble, and the ideal protection plan is one which can adapt itself easily without financial loss to births, deaths, a new job, or changes in the family income or in the number of dependants. Every time you change your mind with a conventional prepaid policy you lose your shirt. Since you have already paid for your later-life protection in advance, it could hardly be otherwise. With the term-savings plan, you can change your mind as often as you like, for the most part without financial loss, and where there is a loss it is only a small fraction of that suffered under a conventional policy.

Every time you buy more term insurance, and at least every five years if you have ceased buying, you should take out the composite graph of your term-savings plan and subject it to a long look. Take yours (Fig. 14) now and look at it. Let us say that twenty years have passed since you made the graph. You are 40, and everything has gone as planned. You have had four children who are protected by a total of nearly $345,000. But in the past ten years there has been another depression. You have suffered some business reversals, and with your decreased income, decreased insurance premiums would be gratifying. Look at your graph and see what would happen if you dropped one of the $50,000 term policies. The line representing the total amount of protection would drop suddenly to below $300,000, but then pick up because of the savings plan until it reached a peak of $315,000 at age 50. When things are tough, this is adequate protection for a family of three, so under the circumstances you drop some of your term insurance and have more money for daily expenses.

## Some Possible Difficulties and Their Solution

### Your health

The term-savings plan depends on your being able to buy cheap life insurance of some kind. When you come to buy term insurance, living in Canada has its disadvantages. In the U.S. people are more wide-awake and better informed on legal rackets, and as a result, there has been public pressure to bring plans for cheap life insurance into effect. Here there is no such pressure as yet, and the companies can get away with more because they have no competition. One point at which they will try to bring pressure to keep you from buying term insurance is through the medical examination. If you are in top physical condition, positively bubbling over with health, the company will not dare to refuse you term insurance on these grounds. But if you are a borderline case, perhaps in good health now, but with a family history of a serious disease, they may try to take this way out.

I have not yet been able to determine whether this practice of refusing to sell term, but offering to sell a standard-rate life policy, is against the law. But, illegal or not, it is done very frequently. The intent of the Canadian and British Insurance Companies Act, 1932, as I read it, seems to be that such a practice is illegal, but I find no definite prohibition. Some day an energetic citizen will bring a company to court on the question, and then we shall know. I am trying to get a grant from the Canada Council to contest such a case, but so far they are holding back.

In the meantime, the question is, what to do if you are refused term insurance on medical grounds? What you do, in order of desirability, is as follows:

*Try Another Canadian Company.* Say you have been refused 10-year term. You pick out the second-best term policy offered. Try this company, mentioning in your application that you were refused term by the other company, but offered a standard-rate whole-life policy. If the second company refuses too:

*Try Another Type of Renewable-Term Policy.* Most companies are much more willing to sell "term to age 65" than 10-year term. Look in the comparison tables in Appendix 4 and choose a company which sells this type. If you have been trying the larger companies, this time try a small one. This term-to-age-65 policy is not very desirable, because it makes you pay for insurance too far in advance, but it is better than convertible term, and much better than ordinary life. If this, too, fails:

*Try Another Province or Country.* If you are in a business that causes you to travel to New York State or Massachusetts or Connecticut, it is fairly easy to take out insurance there. All you have to do is walk into any savings bank and give a local address on the application form. Suppose you have friends in New York City, and go there occasionally on business. Get permission from your friends to use their home as a mailing address, and give this address on your insurance application. The Bowery Savings Bank (like most banks in New York, Connecticut, and Massachusetts) sells term insurance at relatively cheap rates.

## Term Policies with a Medical Rating

If you are not in good health the insurance companies give you what they call a "medical rating", and this determines the amount you have to pay per thousand over and above the regular premium. Depending on how much of a crock you are, the rating will be Class A, B, C, and so on. If you have a medical history of some serious disease, you might be rated Class D.

It may be that a renewable-term policy with a medical rating will be a better bargain for you than any of the other alternatives. The chief companies in Canada selling this kind of insurance are Occidental Life and Dominion Life. The latter is owned by Lincoln National Life in the United States, which specializes in rated policies, hence is in a position to draw on a very wide experience.

A healthy person, age 35, can buy five-year renewable term for $2.86 a thousand. The corresponding premiums for medical ratings A and B respectively are $2.86 plus $1.27, or $4.13; and $2.86 plus $2.53, or $5.39.

On decreasing term the medical-rating system is relatively simple. You take the normal premium and add 25 percent for Class A, 50 percent for Class B, 75 percent for Class C, and so on.

The desirability of this alternative depends entirely on how good a medical rating you can get from the company. If all companies have refused to sell you term at standard rates, and Occidental offers you term with a Class A rating, then this is probably your best buy. If on the other hand you are given a Class D rating, look around some more. You may find that one of the other five alternatives is cheaper. In any case, make your calculations before buying. Only after you have made careful arithmetical calculations of all the policies you are able to buy are you in a position to make an intelligent choice.

If your health is so bad that you can get only special high-rate insurance, your plan will depend on how far you are along in life. If you are young, working, unmarried, and in chronic poor health, you will put all your protection money into a savings plan. This will build up an insurance value quickly; and then, if, after ten or fifteen years, you get married, you will not need to buy insurance at high rates to protect your dependant. You will already be insured by your savings plan. If, on the other hand, you are already married with dependants, but in poor health, the idea is to buy some insurance to create an immediate estate in case you should die, but put as much as possible into your savings.

The savings should always be considered first. It is the bargain package. If in doubt as to whether to put a sum of money into an increased savings plan or increased high-price insurance, choose the savings. Your aim, no matter what your state of health, should be to drop all your life-insurance policies before you are 60. The sooner you can afford to drop your life insurance, the more money you will have to spend on just living.

**Your emotions**

Apart from your health, the factor most likely to cause you trouble when buying insurance is your emotions. The real nature of life insurance is obscured by the emotional values connected with it. The companies and the men who make their modest profits by selling this service are careful to play up the emotional values; hence the flood of advertisements of the type: "Do you want your little children to starve to death? If not, buy an unreconstructed 10-pay policy from us."

If you can wipe the tears of sentiment from your eyes, buying life insurance turns out to be just the same as buying a soft drink. You can buy it by the case, and get it for 15 cents a bottle. Or you can get it (in normal times) for 25 cents at a cheap roadside stand. At most city eating places of the poorer sort you pay 40 cents, and in the places with some pretensions of tone, it costs you perhaps a dollar. At the other end of the scale, if you have it delivered to your hotel room, or drink it in a New York nightclub, the cost is two dollars or more. But, however much you pay, the drink is exactly the same. For a person who likes the taste of this stuff and is not particularly interested in the services which may be given with it, the best way to buy a bottle is to go to a roadside stand. But there is good money to be made in selling a 15-cent article for a dollar, and if you do it often enough you can attain quite a respectable position in society. For this reason there are thousands of people trying to do it.

Life insurance is ideal for this "15 cents to a dollar" type of selling, because it can be easily disguised to look like something it isn't. A mythical benefit here, a pat phrase there, and a plain life-insurance policy becomes something fancy—well worth the extra few dollars a month it costs. Another rule, then, is: Don't let your emotions obscure the nature of the product you are buying. Buy insurance in cold blood, just the way you buy eggs.

One way to keep your emotions in check is to develop an attitude of healthy cynicism when you read insurance-company advertising.

## The Actual Purchase

Now that you know how much of what policy to buy, and from what company, only one point remains. Either you own life insurance now, or you don't. If you are not insured, the rest of the trip is relatively easy. What you do is get the chosen company to send you an application form by mail. You fill it out answering the health-related questions truthfully but without gratuitous detail. During the medical examination (if required), answer the doctor's questions but don't volunteer any information not asked. It's like going through customs. Give the company a check for $\frac{1}{12}$ of the annual premium with the application form. As soon as the company tells you the policy is issued, read it carefully, making sure that everything is laid out in writing. All the RCNP[2] conditions must be in. If all is well, send a check for the remainder of the annual premium to the company, so you won't be charged extra for part payments.

If you own life insurance now, the closing procedure is a little more complicated. Neither the companies nor the agents make much money on term insurance (only up to 300 percent profit each year) and they are loath to sell it. It is a bad type of insurance from the point of view of the company, because the policyholder can drop out of his contract at any time without much financial loss and the company gets little "savings" to play with. The solution to this problem is to buy from a company that sells a lot of term insurance and is accustomed to selling it. A list of such companies would include Equitable Life of Iowa, Occidental, and Dominion.

If you already have a cash-value insurance, and are now trying to change to a sensible plan, the steps are these:

**Step 1**: Ask the salesman to get you a specimen policy, as issued by his company, and ask him to explain any paragraph you do not understand.

**Step 2**: If your health is good, or you have had a medical examination recently which pronounced you healthy, go to the manager of a large city agency (if possible) and tell him you want some one- or five-year renewable term. Do not go to the salesman from whom you bought your other policies. Do not go to a salesman who is a friend, a relative, or a friend of a friend.

**Step 3**: Fill out the application form. The most important question on the application form is the one about twisting. Twisting is the act of *inducing* the policyholder to turn in the policy that is draining him and to replace it with one that gives him twice the protection for half the expense. Many people feel that they have the right to lie on the application form, and when they come to the question "Is this policy being bought to replace any now in force?", they answer "No" with a clear conscience. They argue that they have a perfect right to change their minds later on, since the policy is their own and was bought with their own money.

In 1952, when I was doing insurance consulting on the side, I got a legal opinion on this question from a prominent Montreal law firm. Here it is:

"The question whether an applicant intends to cancel other policies appears to be quite irrelevant and to have no bearing on the appreciation of the risk to be undertaken by the insurance company. Such a question therefore on an application appears improper and we cannot see how a company could justify either refusal to issue a policy if the question was answered in a certain sense, or refusal to pay the amount of the insurance if it turned out that the question had been answered incorrectly."

But there is a difference of opinion even among lawyers as to this question of changing your mind. Some think it disingenuous to answer "No" on the form, when all the time you had the idea of changing the policy fixed in your mind. That was the *reason* for the whole exercise. Perhaps a better solution for some would be the one given by McLeod on page 119 of his *Life Insurance and You*. That is, get your salesman to send a signed copy of the standard notice form to the company whose policy you are cancelling.

However, my impression, after a lifetime of studying this industry, is that, if you answer "Yes" to this question, and put in the proper forms, you may well find that the company refuses to sell you the insurance protection. They will not *say* it is because you answered "Yes", but they will find other grounds for refusal.

If you are a hypochondriac, and enjoy telling others about your diseases, please try to restrain yourself when filling out the application form. The idea is to tell the truth, but make yourself seem as long-lived a person as possible.

One point about which you must be absolutely truthful is your dealings with other insurance companies. The life companies maintain a joint bureau where records are kept of your attempts to get insurance from various companies, and the reports of the company physicians who examined you. Therefore, the answers to these questions must be on the up and up:

1. "Have you applied for insurance within the last 12 months?"
2. "If yes, did you in each case receive a policy for the full amount and plan applied for, at your actual age and at the standard premium?"

**Step 4**: Make out a check for $1/12$ of the annual premium and give it to the agent, who will give you a receipt for it.

**Step 5**: Take your medical examination as quickly as possible after making out the application, to reduce the time in which the insurance company has your money but you have no legally binding protection. True, the application forms of many companies say that the policy is in force from the date of application; but the fact remains that the company has the right to reject any application. It might just possibly decide that a cadaver is not a good insurance risk.

Do not volunteer any information to the doctor. Answer only the question he asks. Arrange to have the examination in the morning, after a light breakfast, rather than in the afternoon after a heavy lunch, when your heart is working hard trying to digest the food. Do not drink soft drinks the night before.

**Step 6**: When the policy is delivered, subtract the amount of your first check from the total annual premium, and give the salesman a check for the difference. By giving them a small amount to start, you tie up a minimum amount of money if the application is refused; and on the other hand, you do not incur the extra charges made by companies for half-yearly, quarterly, or monthly payments.

**Step 7**: After the policy is delivered, read it carefully. An insurance policy has been defined as a document which gives you all sorts of rights in large print on the front page, and then takes them all away in fine print on the back. So read your policy carefully, and see the manager immediately about anything you don't understand. Some important points to check are these:

### Contestability

In a way peculiar to insurance companies, the contestability clause is always labeled "incontestability clause". Whatever they call it, make sure it is there. This clause of your policy should say that after the policy has been in effect for two years, the only reason it can be cancelled is that you have failed to pay the premium. In other words, after the two years the policy is yours for as long as you want to keep it (up to age 65), no matter what you have said in the application.

### Renewability

Your whole protection plan depends on this, so make sure it is written down in the policy. "The policyholder is free to renew the policy without medical examination at any time before his 65th year." This sentence, or one like it, must be in your policy or your plan is useless. Make certain that the phrase "without medical examination" is not merely implied, but is written down in black and white. The rates at which the contract may be renewed at any age should form part of the policy.

### Period of grace

Most policies allow you thirty days after the due date each year to make your payment of premium. Make sure that this period of grace is allowed without interest; that is, that you do not have to pay interest on your premium if you are some days late in paying it.

Try not to sign a policy which binds you to keep on paying premiums after your death. If you pay your premium in January, that pays your insurance for the whole year. If you die in February of that year the company should return $^{11}/_{12}$ of the premium to your widow, because obviously you do not need to be insured for the rest of the year.

A more specific recommendation is this: never sign an application for a policy on the same day that you have talked about it with the salesman. Wait a week if possible, and allow the effect of the salesman's personality to wear off. Then read the specimen policy you have asked the salesman to send you, and make sure you understand all its conditions. Finally, reread all the conditions of the application very carefully, making sure that the policy fits your needs, and that you can't buy the same thing cheaper somewhere else. Then, and only then, sign the application and mail it in.

# Chapter 6 Finding the Real Cost of Your Insurance and Learning the Twist

*From the standpoint of the degree of refinement, the yield method appears to be superior to all three of the methods previously described. Not only does it recognize interest, which is ignored in the traditional method, but also it recognizes the declining amount of protection in level-premium policies, which is not considered in any of the other three methods.*
      JOSEPH M. BELTH
      *Life Insurance: A Consumer's Handbook*, p. 16

Joseph M. Belth, a life-insurance executive who is now a professor at Indiana University (see Bibliography), has written a book making elaborate comparisons of prices for various types of insurance. He describes six different methods, most of which require the use of a main-frame computer. It is good to see progress in this vexed question of price comparison. At least we are getting away from the juvenile analysis that doesn't even allow for the fact that money earns interest. But, on the other hand, why do it? The difference in price between term and ordinary life during the first twenty years is so great you can prove it best by counting on your fingers. After 30 years the situation changes, as the prices of the two types come together, and at 40 years they can be very close. But by this time the real question is not how much does it cost, but: "Do I need insurance protection at *all*?" Even if you have spent or lost all your savings plan money, all is not lost. As I have mentioned, except under the most unusual circumstances your forty-year-old children do not need your earnings to survive.

## A Note About Insurance-Company Actuaries and Executives

This book is highly critical of the way life-insurance companies operate. Therefore, to protect their companies and their jobs, insurance executives will set some high-priced help feverishly to work to find flaws in it. If they can find a mistake, an inadvertency, an inconsistency, or a typographical error among the thousands of figures in this book, then they can point to it with pride, and imply that all the other figures given are equally false.

Before you accept a rebuttal based on such a discovery, you should read the following discussion of the problem involved in comparing different policies and savings plans. It will tell you why several sets of premium rates are used in the book, some dating back forty years.

## The Degree of Accuracy Required

Insurance policies of different companies can be compared at many different levels of accuracy. To get the difference in value correct to the last cent, you have to have a main-frame computer, an electronic calculator, a library of books and tables, plenty of leisure time, and a good actuarial mind. Most of us lack one or more of these requirements, and therefore our comparisons of policies cannot be accurate to the penny.

But the differences between policies are so great that this degree of accuracy is seldom necessary. If one company charges $3,000 a year for the protection you can get from another for $300, you will buy the second policy and not worry about the odd cent or the odd dollar in your calculations.

The thing to remember is this: a quick comparison of policies is never accurate, because in actuarial science speed and accuracy are mutually exclusive. This is because speed is obtained by the use of approximations—and approximations are only approximate. The method to use in comparing policies is first to try a simple method of comparison using approximations. If the two policies turn out to be vastly different under this method, you will be safe in buying the cheaper one without comparing the two further. If, on the other hand, they turn out about the same, you must try a more accurate method of comparison, using fewer approximations. For maximum accuracy you will have to use no approximations at all, and go through a tedious set of calculations. But this degree of accuracy is seldom needed.

### What Is a Fair Term Rate to Use?

Remember too that there isn't a single comparison that can't be objected to on some grounds. For instance, what term rate is fair to use in these examples? There are some objections to every one.

| Rate | Objection |
|---|---|
| 1. Lowest premium yearly renewable non-participating term | Not the cheapest rate. |
| 2. Cheapest decreasing-term rate for any given age | The protection decreases every year. |
| 3. Five-year-term participating | Dividends are never guaranteed. You have to start by paying an excessive premium. |
| 4. Net rates which record my actual twenty-year experience with Metropolitan term | The new buyer has to start today, not forty years ago. Insurance rates have dropped since 1943. |
| 5. Average of the five-year-term policies available | One-year term is often cheaper. |

The old question, "Fair's fair, but what's fair?" comes up continually in comparing life-insurance policies. If you compare the worst possible term policy with the best possible cash-value policy, the amount available for savings each year is not going to be much. On the other hand, if you take the best term policy and compare it with the worst cash-value policy, the savings are spectacular. If you take the average price of recognized term policies, and compare it with the average premium of recognized cash-value policies, we would seem to have a fair comparison, but of course you can't buy averages.

At a given age (say 20), the rates for different kinds of term insurance range from fifty cents to $11.31 per thousand, and the rates for different kinds of cash-value insurance are even worse, ranging from $9 for ordinary life to $109 for a 10-year endowment. With such a range in prices, averages tend to be meaningless.

In addition, it makes a big difference whether you buy $1,000 or $300,000 worth of term, because many companies add a service charge for each policy, and, in addition, volume buying is cheaper. Moreover, there are special policies set up by the companies from time to time just to get a particular piece of business. These rates do not appear in any printed work.

This may sound like nit-picking, but the first thing a salesman is going to say when someone tries to change his insurance is that I have falsified the comparisons by using unrealistic premiums for the policies compared.

### What Is a Fair Cash-Value Rate to Use?

When you are 20, the premium for $1,000 of insurance protection in a cash-value policy can be anything from $9 to $109. If you already have such a policy, you use the rates you are actually paying. If you are not insured, use both the highest and the lowest rate to assure yourself that, even using the lowest rate, separating your savings from your insurance is better.

### Should You Use Old or New Rates?

Life-insurance premiums are constantly decreasing, and annuity rates are constantly increasing, both because people are living longer. If you use old rates, "dividends" can be accurately figured, but you can't buy at those rates any more. If you use new rates that you can buy, you must guess about "dividends".

### Should You Use Participating or Non-Participating Rates?

Non-participating is simpler, and the figures are guaranteed. But if you choose non-participating as the basis of an argument with an insurance agent, he will say you have deliberately chosen high-priced policies to make the business look bad.

### Treatment of "Dividends"

Your choices are:

—Compare policies of the same company so the "dividends" are the same percentage of premiums.
—Ignore them, because they can be stopped at any time and often are.

—Use old policies so you can make use of actual dividend histories.
—Use the company's estimate of dividends to come.

## What Is the Nature of the Savings Portion?

If you take large risks with your savings portion you may have a very
fast rate of growth. If you insist on a guaranteed return, you may have
to be satisfied with only 4 percent tax-free.

## What Is Your Tax Bracket?

In Canada you can pay the government anything from 14 percent to
50 percent of your taxable income. How much you actually earn on
your investments is determined in large part by your tax bracket.

## What Is a Fair Interest Rate to Use for the Savings Portion?

Interest rates depend on many factors, some too complex to be
outlined here. But the least you can earn with your money at the
moment is the 9 percent paid by the savings banks, or the 12 percent
you can get on government bonds. Of course, you have to pay income
tax on the interest earned, so you won't net 12 percent. If, for
example, you pay out in taxes an average of 25 percent of what you
earn, your net return will be 9 percent.

## Twisting

When you finally prove to yourself that you have been sold too much
of the wrong kind of insurance at a fancy price by a salesman who is no
longer in the business, what do you do? What you do is twist. You buy
a policy that suits *your* needs, not the salesman's, and then you turn in
your old policy and collect the cash-surrender value.

As you might expect, the insurance companies have long since had
their friends in government arrange the law, so twisting is illegal. This
is not to say twisting isn't done, but only that you should take certain
precautions while doing it. I have been an accessory before the fact on
twisting cases for forty years, and I have never had a case go sour. In
fact they all resulted in large profits for the client, and some were
absolutely spectacular.

Beginning with the earliest, here is a twist I worked out for a
wealthy doctor in 1943. He had been loaded up with expensive life
insurance by an enterprising salesman, and when I came on the scene
he was rejoicing in $54,000 worth of protection that had a cash value

of $20,000. I got him to replace this nonsense with twice as much protection ($100,000) in decreasing term, at a cost of $578 instead of $2,264. Each year, the saving of $1,686 was put into a portfolio of convertible bonds and preferred stocks, which has shown a net growth rate of 6 percent after taxes, counting both income and capital gain. The $20,000 cash value was put into State Street Investment Corporation, a mutual fund, at $19.65 a share, buying just over 1,000 shares.

By 1962 the State Street was worth (in asset value, plus value of shares received as dividends) $146.37 a share, and in addition paid a dividend of over $3,000 a year on his holding.

The results of this change from cash-value plan to term-savings plan were as follows at the end of 40 years:

The client has dropped all conventional insurance, and is completely self-insured. The savings plan is now valued at:

1. The $1,686 a year saved in premiums mounted
   up at 3% for 40 years to make (after taxes)        $127,126
2. The mutual fund is now worth                        305,000
                Grand and glorious total              $432,126

One crowning touch: instead of paying $2,264 to the insurance company each year, this man receives $3,000 dividends on his mutual fund!

Here is a poor magazine writer who had no scruples about investing in life-insurance stocks with the savings portion of his own term-savings plan. In 1947 he had $5,000 of protection in 20-pay life that was costing him $149 a year. I had him buy $10,000 of Metropolitan 10-year renewable term, because I thought he was underinsured. This cost him an average of $4.50 per thousand a year for the period, so he saved $104 a year in premiums by buying twice as much protection. The cash value received when the policies were turned in was just over $1,000.

Sixteen years later, he was adequately self-insured through his own investments, and could drop the insurance if he liked. I don't know what happened to the $104 a year. It was supposed to go into a government annuity, but I think he spent it. So we will ignore that item.

But the cash value alone, invested in a portfolio of life-insurance stocks, provided enough for his financial peace of mind. It was worth just over $100,000!

It is true that the forties were the ideal time to cash insurance policies and invest in mutual funds or common stocks. There has been a tremendous rise in the market, and this has led to some spectacular gains. But even without such eye-popping results, the term-savings plan makes sense whether the investment of the savings is successful or not and whether the client lives or dies.

Another case, about 1945, featured a client who didn't want to take any risk with his insurance money. He knew all about common stocks, and how they had dropped during the depression, and wanted no part of them. But he did have a $3,000 cash value in his insurance policy. I persuaded him that he would always need a place to live, and that the $80 a month he was paying for his apartment was money more or less down the drain. This argument appealed to him, so he got his cash value, took out term insurance to protect his wife, and bought a nice little bungalow for $3,000 cash and a mortgage of $2,000. Today the house is worth $120,000, and the mortgage has been paid off painlessly in place of rent.

In 1957 I had a client who seriously questioned whether it was possible to earn more than insurance-company or bank interest with the savings portion of the term-savings plan. The market seemed to be at the top of a long rise, real estate seemed overpriced, and it did appear difficult to place money so it would earn good post-tax income.

I persuaded him to go along with the term-savings plan on the strength of what would happen if he died. In this eventuality, his estate would have not only the face value of the term policy, but the cash value of $3,335 from turning in the old policy and the annual savings of $361 on premiums.

But no one can predict the future. What actually happened was that we put the entire cash value and the first four years' savings into American Growth Fund. Today the total investment of $3,335 plus $1,444 (4 × $361) has grown to nearly $100,000.

In all the above cases I am able to say exactly what happened because they are in the past. The case that follows is more recent, hence the only thing that is certain is, if the policyholder dies, his heirs will be better off under the term-savings plan than they would have been under the old plan. At the very least, we have rescued the savings portion, so it will not be confiscated when the policyholder dies.

Here is a man who had been sold great gobs of expensive endowment insurance against the day of his retirement. But the way it worked out was the poor client had to work harder than ever to pay the premiums, and it was the salesman who retired, on the commissions. The premiums were $30 a thousand for the first ten years, then $60 a thousand for the next ten, and finally $117 a thousand. I had him buy his pure insurance protection at $5.45 a thousand, thus saving $1,150 a year in premiums, besides recovering $2,260 in cash value. As I wrote to his former "estate planner", who had come out of retirement to send me a disgruntled letter:

"By spending exactly the same amount for annual premiums, we have a choice between your plan (1) and mine (2). The following table shows how the two plans work out for the three possible eventualities, for different periods:

| Year | Client dies. His heirs receive: | | Client lives. Liquid capital on hand: | | Client lives but gives up protection: | |
| | Plan 1 | Plan 2 | Plan 1 | Plan 2 | Plan 1 | Plan 2 |
|---|---|---|---|---|---|---|
| 1960 | $37,000 | $70,419 | 0 | $ 3,419 | $2,260 | $ 3,419 |
| 1965 | 37,000 | 67,550 | 0 | 9,550 | | 9,550 |
| 1970 | 37,000 | 67,750 | 0 | 19,250 | 3,760 | 19,250 |
| 1975 | 37,000 | 68,000 | 0 | 32,200 | | 32,200 |
| 1980 | 37,000 | 72,400 | 0 | 49,800 | 6,740 | 49,800 |
| 1985 | 37,000 | 79,700 | 0 | 72,700 | | 72,700 |

[**Table 14.** *Comparison of a standard insurance company plan (1) with a "buy-term-and-invest-the-difference" plan (2)*

"Of course, these figures depend in part upon the client's being able to earn 6 percent after taxes, in income and capital gain, on his invested funds. With trust companies offering 13 percent mortgage pools, I feel that this is not an unreasonable goal today."

### The Real Cost of Your Insurance

**Your money earns interest for somebody, if not for you**

Cash is a revenue-producing asset. If you have cash, you can always make it earn money for you. As I have stressed, this is one fact you have to keep in mind when figuring how much a life-insurance plan is costing you each year. If the insurance company is holding $10,000 of your money, in the form of the cash-surrender value of the policy or in retained "dividends", you are losing the interest that this money is earning each year. This interest must be added to the apparent cost of your insurance (the premium) in order to find the true cost of the protection.

**How your tax rate affects the rate of interest earned**

Just how much you are losing in interest each year depends on your income-tax bracket and what tax shelters you have been able to arrange for your income. The "savings" part of a cash-value life-insurance policy earns about 2½ percent tax-free. But other types of investment earn more, and there are many other tax shelters. Here is a simplified table showing alternatives if you have $20,000 to invest.

| Plan: | Tax-free amount |
|---|---|
| 1. Buy insurance. Of the $20,000 premium, $10,000 is the savings part. 2½% of this is | $ 250 |
| 2. Buy $20,000 worth of stock that pays a 5% dividend ($1,000) | $1,000 |
| 3. With $20,000 cash buy a $100,000 building. 5% depreciation allowance* | $5,000 |
| 4. With $20,000 cash buy a $20,000 building (no mortgage, therefore little risk). 5% depreciation allowance* | $1,000 |

*While part of this depreciation allowance must be used to pay for natural wear and tear on the building, this is often offset by a rising market price caused by inflation.

**Table 15.** *Alternative tax shelters*

For the examples in this book I normally use the rock-bottom interest rate of 6 percent, since this is the amount anyone can net tax-free (see p. 81). A 10 percent rate would be fairer, and sometimes I use this rate. If you want to give any weight at all to capital gain in your calculations, a 12 percent rate is not unreasonable.

### How to analyse your present policy

To find out what your insurance is really costing you each year, substitute the appropriate figures in the following calculation. The example used is a participating whole-life policy issued to a client at age 39 by North American Life.

---

**1. The situation now:**

| | | |
|---|---:|---:|
| Face value | | $10,000 |
| Less cash value, | | 870 |
| or co-insurance | | |
| Actual insurance protection | | $ 9,130 |
| Gross annual premium | $229.90 | |
| Subtract Dividend | 16.20 | |
| Apparent net premium | $213.70 | |
| Add interest loss on cash | | |
| value, at 6% | 52.50 | |
| Actual premium | $266.20 | |

Therefore actual cost of your insurance this year is $\frac{266.20}{9,130.00}$ or $29 per $1,000.

---

**2. The situation 10 years from now:**

| | | |
|---|---:|---:|
| Face value | | $10,000 |
| Less cash value, or | | |
| co-insurance | | 2,760 |
| Actual insurance protection | | $ 7,240 |
| Gross annual premium | $229.90 | |
| Dividend | 16.50 | |
| Apparent net premium | $213.40 | |
| Interest loss on cash value, | | |
| at 6% | 165.60 | |
| Actual premium | $379.00 | |

Therefore actual cost of your insurance in 10th year is $\frac{379}{7240}$, or $52 per $1,000.

**Table 16.** *Actual cost per $1,000 of a participating whole-life policy*

Do the same for 20- and 30-year periods, to prove to yourself that the premium per thousand rises constantly.

Here is another example, using a 20-year endowment bought at age 40 from Metropolitan Life. Let us see the cost at the end of 1, 5, 10, and 20 years, and compare it with term insurance:

| | Face amount of policy | Cash value (co-insurance) | Company's net risk | Apparent premium | Interest on loans | Total premium per year | Cost of insurance per $1,000 | Cost of equal amount of term protection |
|---|---|---|---|---|---|---|---|---|
| 1st year | $1,000 | $      0 | $1,000 | $53.60 | none | $53.60 | $  53.60 | $  9.09 |
| 5th year | 1,000 | 200 | 800 | 53.60 | none | 53.60 | 67.00 | 10.91 |
| 10th year | 1,000 | 427 | 573 | 53.60 | none | 53.60 | 93.54 | 14.02 |
| 20th year | 1,000 | 1,000 | 0 | 53.60 | none | 53.60 | infinite | 29.87 |

Now consider this same policy if you had been foolish enough to borrow on it to the full extent of the cash value:

| | Face amount of policy | Cash value (co-insurance) | Company's net risk | Apparent premium | Interest on loans | Total premium per year | Cost of insurance per $1,000 | Cost of equal amount of term protection |
|---|---|---|---|---|---|---|---|---|
| 10th year | 1,000 | 427 | 573 | 53.60 | 25.62 | 79.22 | 138.23 | 14.02 |
| 15th year | 1,000 | 670 | 330 | 53.60 | 40.20 | 93.80 | 284.24 | 19.59 |

**Table 17.** *Actual cost per $1,000 of a Metropolitan 20-year endowment*

This table has been simplified by omitting:

1. Dividends paid by the company (which will reduce the premiums).

2. Interest on the cash value (a loss to the policyholder).

3. The cumulative interest on the yearly overpayments (an additional loss to the policyholder).

When all the facts are considered, the results are even more striking. But for all ordinary purposes, the above table is striking enough.

# Chapter 7 Preparing to Battle the Insurance Salesman

*To things of sale a seller's praise belongs.*
SHAKESPEARE, *Love's Labour's Lost*

In any commercial transaction, buyer and seller are opposed. In this chapter I am telling you, the buyer, how to deal with the life-insurance salesman, who is the seller. Therefore, in this chapter, and to some extent throughout the book, the salesman has to be the villain.

But don't get me wrong. Some of my best friends...et cetera; and besides, I don't underestimate the importance of the salesman in our mass-production and mass-waste society. Moreover, insurance men, even if they oversell the wrong kinds of insurance to the wrong people, do *some* good, because often they are the poor man's only source of financial advice.

Insurance salesmen are to some extent themselves the victims of their companies and of the agency system. For the hundreds of salesmen who are sincerely trying to provide their clients with maximum lifetime protection at minimum cost—those who are serious about their work as estate planners—this book provides a solid and thoroughly tested base for operations.

Most insurance salesmen will try to talk you out of buying pay-as-you-go policies for the simple reason that they make less money on this type. Their only recompense is their commission; and, like anyone else, they have to eat. The larger the premium, the more money the salesman makes. When you try to buy a type of insurance which carries low premiums, you are snatching the bread out of the mouths of his children. He cannot be expected to enjoy this, and will go to any lengths to avoid selling you term insurance. The commission earned by the salesman when he sells you "permanent" insurance is both a larger percentage of the premium, and larger in absolute amount, because the premiums are higher. Companies vary, but I have seen salesmen's first-year commissions on term policies ranging from 20 percent to 40 percent of the premium; and first-year commissions on "permanent" insurance ranging from a low of 60 percent to a high of 110 percent. These two factors combine to make a tremendous difference between what the salesman gets for himself when he sells you term insurance and what he gets when he sells you prepaid insurance.

But even using just *one* of the factors, and taking the same percentage rate of return for the two kinds of policies (60 percent), the differences are spectacular enough.

| | | Agent's commission | | | |
|---|---|---|---|---|---|
| Premium | Type of policy | 1st year | 2nd year | 3rd to 10th year | Total |
| $974 | 10-year endowment | $584 | $146 | $48.70 × 8 = $390 | $1,120. |
| 356 | 20-pay life | 213 | 53 | 18 × 8 = 144 | 410. |
| 237 | Ordinary life | 142 | 36 | 12 × 8 = 96 | 274. |
| 19 | One-year term | 11 | 3 | 1 × 8 = 8 | 22. |

(All policies are for $10,000, taken out at age 30.)

**Table 18.** *Why the salesman does not want to sell term insurance*

A glance at Table 18 will show you why you carry the kind of insurance you do. The object of this book is to tell you explicitly how to get the tattered remnants of your shirt back.

Another reason why you will have to fight to buy term insurance is that the insurance companies do not make nearly so much money on it as they do on prepaid policies. Moreover, they have less of your money to play with. The salesman who makes a habit of selling it is likely to get into trouble with his company.

## The Salesman's Arguments

Depending on his estimate of your intelligence, the insurance salesman uses one or more of the following arguments to keep you from buying term insurance:

## The net-cost argument

If the agent thinks you have a dull look, he will start off with the phony cost exhibit. He adds the bare premiums paid over 20 years, subtracts the then cash value of the policy, and says the difference is the actual cost of the insurance to you. This often turns out to be zero. In other words, all this time you have had your insurance protection for nothing! To demolish this argument, all you have to remember is that money earns interest and you have been grossly overpaying for years.

Over forty years ago I published an article explaining how the life-insurance business really operated. All the financial wizards who were in sympathy with the life companies immediately jumped on the article in an attempt to discredit it. Wellington Jeffers, then financial editor of the Toronto *Globe and Mail*, devoted a whole column to showing how my article was misleading. I have nothing to add to what I said then, which went in part like this:

> The review of my articles on the life insurance business by Wellington Jeffers, financial editor of the *Globe and Mail*, used the stock argument of the life companies: the phony "cost exhibit". He sees the obvious fact that my plan makes use of term insurance. This must be so, because term insurance is the nearest thing to pure life insurance available today. He then proceeds to compare the net cost of term and ordinary life insurance, using the cost exhibit that agents use to fool yokels:

|  | Term insurance | Ordinary life insurance |
|---|---|---|
| Total premium at age 65 (begun at age 30) | $800 | $805 |
| Cash value at age 65 | nil | 550 |
| Net cost of insurance | $800 | $255 |

[**Table 19.** *Life insurance according to Wellington Jeffers*]

> Now the point that has here escaped Mr. Jeffers is one that every financial editor should know, that is, that money earns interest. If you buy a house for $8,000 cash, you do not henceforth live in it for nothing

but pay out as rent an amount equal to the interest your money would have earned had it been invested at 4 percent. In other words, before you pay any expenses of taxes, upkeep, and depreciation, your house is costing $320 a year. Similarly, over-payments made on an insurance premium will earn interest if invested elsewhere. The following table [Table 20] is a more genuine cost exhibit, showing the difference between representative term and ordinary life policies.

| 1 | 2 | 3 | 4 | 5 | 6 | 7 |
|---|---|---|---|---|---|---|
| | | Rates (to nearest 50¢ per $1,000) | | | | |
| Age | Years elapsed since policy was taken out | Term 10-year renewable | Ordinary life | Difference in premiums; i.e. amount available for investment per year (overpayment) | Amount of difference (Col. 5) for 10 years at 4% compounded annually | The amount (Col. 6) earns interest at 4% compounded annually and becomes: |
| 25 | 0 | $ 9 | $21 | $12 | $144 | $467 (30 yrs.) |
| 35 | 10 | 11 | 21 | 10 | 120 | 263 (20 yrs.) |
| 45 | 20 | 18 | 21 | 3 | 36 | 43 (10 yrs.) |
| | | | | | | $783 |
| | | | | | | −108 |
| 55 | 30 | 30 | 21 | −9 | −108 | 675 |
| 65 | 40 | | | | | |

| | Term | Ordinary |
|---|---|---|
| Total premium to age 65 | $680 | $ 840 |
| Overpayments and interest | nil | 675 |
| | $680 | $1,515 |
| Cash surrender value | | 550 |
| Net cost | 680 | 965 |

[Table 20. Comparison of Metropolitan term insurance with ordinary life (ignoring dividends, which are the same for both). 1945 rates.]

The premium paid for insurance is divided into two parts, the amount required to pay for pure insurance, and the amount to be set aside as savings. Since in a term policy there are no savings, the term premium may be considered the cost of insurance at a given age. Any premium above this amount must be considered savings. The only way to make a meaningful cost exhibit is to compare two definite policies at a definite age. To a customer at age 25, Metropolitan offers 10-year renewable term at $9 a thousand, and ordinary life at $21 a thousand. Both these amounts are gross premiums for participating policies, and would be reduced by dividends. But since the dividends are about the same for both policies, they can be neglected.

For the first 10-year period, the difference between the two premiums is $12; for the second 10-year period, $10; for the third, $3; and for the last 10-year period, the term premium is larger than the other by $9. If you buy ordinary life, you leave these amounts invested with the company, and at age 65 are able to surrender the policy and recover $550. If you buy term insurance and invest the amounts saved in premiums at 4 percent, at age 65 the savings will have grown to $675 per thousand.

From the above it is apparent that term insurance is superior to ordinary life as an investment. The difference of $285 is what you save if you live. If you die, under the term plan your beneficiary receives $1,000 from the insurance company and $675 from the investment, for a total of $1,675. Under the ordinary life plan your beneficiaries receive $1,000 and the savings disappear. Since these results are somewhat at variance with insurance-company advertising, I would not have the reader take my word for them. I would refer him to a source which even Mr. Jeffers will consider impeccable—no idealistic dreaming scholar, but an experienced man of affairs. This is one Valentine Howell, vice-president and actuary of the Prudential Insurance Company of America. He writes:

"The practice of showing the net cost as the difference between the net payments and the cash surrender value is a usual one in life-insurance circles, in spite of its theoretical incorrectness and absurd results. By it, the 'net cost' of endowment contracts can often be shown to be less than nothing; and if the interest basis used in the computation of premiums and reserves is reduced to 2½ percent, as has recently been done in my own company, the increase in the cash surrender value at the end of twenty years more than offsets the increase in the net payments so that the 'net cost' appears lower than before, although the reverse is actually the case." (*Canadian Forum*, April 1945, p. 18)

## Permanent insurance

The next thing the salesman will bring up is the idea of "permanent" insurance. He will say that most term insurance ends at age 65 (though the fact is that some policies go to age 100); but far from being a drawback, this is one of its best features. As I've discussed earlier, would you pay for fire insurance on your house eighty years in advance? When you buy "permanent" (i.e. prepaid) insurance, you are doing just this. You are paying insurance on your bodily house to age 100, without considering that it will be destroyed long before this. Moreover, insurance is to protect dependants. How many people do you expect to have dependent on you at age 85? Even your senile son of 65 will be a pensioner by then.

## Constantly rising premiums

If the first two barrels misfire, the salesman will next warn you that the premiums for term insurance keep increasing as you grow older, and finally they will become so high that you will be unable to buy any insurance at all. Before succumbing to this frightening picture, take a look at Table 21. It shows that up to any reasonable age the cost of term insurance never approaches that of other plans.

And this is not the whole story on rising premiums. The time it takes for term premiums to rise to the level of the pre-payment plans

| Age | Yearly renewable term to age 100 | Ordinary life | 20-pay life |
|-----|------|------|------|
| 20 | $ 1 | $14 | $24 |
| 30 | 2 | 19 | 28 |
| 40 | 3 | 26 | 37 |
| 50 | 7 | 39 | 48 |
| 60 | 19 | 62 | 68 |

The amounts shown under Ordinary life and 20-pay life are level premiums for policies taken out at the ages indicated. That is, a man who takes out an ordinary life policy at age 20 pays $14 a year for the life of the policy; at age 40 he pays $26 a year, and so on.

**Table 21.** *How the premiums for all policies rise as you get older. 1982 rates.*

is actually much longer than thirty years. This is because of the co-insurance factor, which is discussed below.

From this you can see that the premiums for term insurance do not rise nearly so rapidly as the salesman would have you believe, and they never reach a point where they give you less for your money than the prepaid plans.

### "Cash surrender value" or co-insurance

This is one of the most amusing things about the life-insurance business as practised. A high cash value is used by most companies as a selling point for their policies, while in fact the higher the cash value the more the policyholder loses. You do not have to be an Einstein to figure this out for yourself. Consider a 20-pay life policy taken out at age 30. It is for $100,000 and the premium is $3,560 a year. After 10 years the cash value is $25,800. This is the amount of your "savings" in the policy. If you die at this time, the company takes your "savings" of $25,800 and adds $74,200 of its own money to make a total of $100,000. This is the money paid to your widow. Since your "savings" are being used to pay part of the death benefit, clearly you have insured yourself. The amount for which you have insured yourself is called co-insurance, and is always exactly the same as the cash value. Co-insurance is the correct name for cash value, but it is a name seldom used by insurance men.

The actual cost of your insurance rises each year (see dotted line, Fig. 17). At the tenth year you are paying $2,939 for $74,200 worth of insurance, which works out at a rate of $39.50 per $1,000. True, your widow will get $100,000 if you die, but $25,800 of this is your own money. (Compare this to the $100,000 of term insurance plus your savings of $25,800 that she would get if you followed my plan.) The company's risk in you (and this is what you pay premiums for) is only $74,200. At the 20th year, your cash value has become so great that the company's risk in you is only $37,700, and yet you are paying $2,490 a year for this protection, or at a rate of $660 per $1,000. After the 20th year the curve rises rapidly to infinity. This is because (although you *seem* to have stopped paying premiums on the 20-pay life) you are still paying about $2,490 a year in the form of 4 percent interest on your then cash value of $62,300. But…the company's risk in you soon drops to zero. Therefore, the actual

**Figure 17**  How Cash Value Decreases Your Insurance Protection

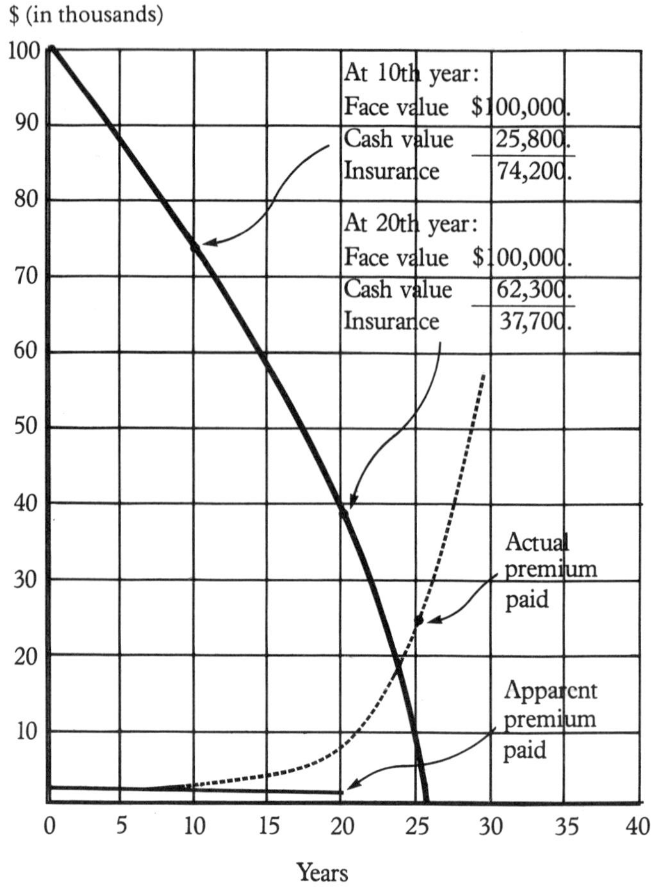

$ (in thousands)

At 10th year:
Face value  $100,000.
Cash value  25,800.
Insurance  74,200.

At 20th year:
Face value  $100,000.
Cash value  62,300.
Insurance  37,700.

Actual premium paid

Apparent premium paid

Years

premium you are paying for $100,000 worth of protection jumps to
$25,000 at the 25th year, and thereafter rises out of sight!

All this sounds like a joke, and from one point of view (the
company's) it is. It is a very humorous joke on you. So, after you finish
laughing, take a look at the insurance policy you are paying for.
Chances are it is a 20-pay life. But if it isn't, remember that the
figures in the graph above apply to any policy which has a cash-
surrender value. You lose slightly less on an ordinary life policy,
slightly more on an endowment policy; but you still lose.

### Decline in health

This is not a very good argument, but it is often heard. The salesman will say that an ordinary policy gives you protection which cannot be taken from you under any circumstances. But any renewable term policy gives you the same thing. Term protection ceases at age 100, which is long enough for anyone. If you fear a decline in health, it is more important than ever to buy term, because at age 30 you can get $190,000 worth of term insurance for the same premium as $10,000 worth of 20-pay life. This gives you an option on $190,000 worth of insurance for life instead of an option on $10,000 for life.

### Decline in earnings

People will sometimes say that you had better pay for insurance years in advance because young men earn more and are better able to pay premiums. This is simply not true. Young and strong road laborers earn more than old and decrepit ones, but the average man in business or industry has a better income after forty years than before. Union men achieve more seniority, civil servants move into higher classifications, simply by the passage of time. Even capitalists amass more capital.

Do not scrimp when you are young to pay for insurance to protect hypothetical dependants when you are old.

### Relative inconvenience

By this time the agent is going to have a vague notion that you know something about insurance, and will begin on the more esoteric arguments. One of these is that term insurance takes some looking after. When you buy 20-pay or ordinary life, you just have to keep on paying the premium every year and think no more about it. With term you have to go to the trouble of renewing it. The answer to this is that renewing term is no trouble at all. You just send the printed notice back to the company along with a check for the next year's premium, and the whole thing is done automatically. But even if it were a great deal of trouble, the money saved would make it worth while.

### Long-term argument

A really smart salesman, who respects your abilities, will probably come in on this tack: *If* you are certain you are not going to die for at least 25 years, and *if* you are sure you will never need to borrow on your policy and will always be able to keep up the premium payments, and *if* you choose the right interest rate, mortality rate, and lapse rate, then it is possible to show that *some* ordinary life policies compare favorably with a term plan as a long-term investment. But, in the first place, the three if's at the beginning are big ones, because if you are certain you are going to live, why go to the expense of carrying insurance at all? If you die holding a prepaid policy of any kind, you lose your investment. The conditions required to win with the best possible bargain in ordinary life are so remote as to be considered impossibilities. You must live for at least 25 years after taking out the policy; you must then cancel the policy and get the cash-surrender value, which leaves you without insurance protection. If you fail to live up to either of these conditions, you lose.

### Some More Subtle Arguments

When the salesman has exhausted all his arguments against term insurance, he will try another tack, and make an attempt to undermine the principle of separating savings from insurance.

### "Not worth the trouble"

In working this line, the salesman recites something like this: "Mr. Prospect, you are a busy man. Top executive time is worth real money. I admit that, by spending a lot of time and money obtaining rates for a dozen different kinds of policies from the hundreds of companies licensed to write insurance, you might finally, after a lot of work, come out with a plan that would save you a few dollars. But is it worth it?" The answer to this argument is in three parts:

(a) It does not take long to compare rates and policies when there is a book like this on the market.

(b) The savings are not "a few dollars" but several hundreds of dollars each year, maybe thousands.

(c) It *is* worth it.

### The social-service argument

This argument, if it is spoken quickly, often sounds quite reasonable. The salesman intones that people are terrible spendthrifts, and if they are not forced by a definite contract to save money, they will never do it. The ordinary life-insurance contract forces people to save money, because they will lose their insurance protection if they do not pay the premiums. In other words, the life companies are doing the country a service in forcing thoughtless citizens to save. But before we cheer this great advance in civilized living, let's take a look at these "savings". The so-called savings of the prepaid or endowment policy is the cash value. The company takes this cash value if you die, and the only way you can get it is by surrendering the policy and going without insurance. This is a queer kind of savings.

Moreover, as a method of saving, life insurance simply doesn't work. The average life of a policy in Canada is seven years. This means that the vast majority of long-term savings plans fail.

This forced-savings argument is the one to which intelligent insurance men such as heads of large agencies invariably retreat when they see that they are speaking to someone who has studied insurance. When I taught at Cornell, the business administration had the same idea. Although the working year was only eight months, they divided our yearly salary into twelve parts, and paid it out one part a month. Thus, men who, after eight years of college and four additional years of teaching experience, were hired at $300 a month were invariably pained to find only $200 in their monthly pay check. The administration justified this dodge by the argument that professors were so stupid that if they were paid all they earned in the eight working months, they would put nothing aside for the summer, and be unable to live. By withholding one-third of each man's earnings for eight months, the trustees were able to keep the professors from starvation, and also to make money for themselves. In this particular university, with a yearly payroll of six million dollars, this scheme cost the employees about $46,000 in lost interest (at 6 percent) each year. This amount was the university's reward for helping the professors who couldn't take care of themselves.

### Yield of investments

Life salesmen used to argue that it was difficult for the ordinary man to earn 4 percent after taxes on his savings. This argument is no longer heard, because trust companies are offering five-year savings certificates yielding 12 percent. Now that the highest individual tax bracket is a mere 50 percent, the lowest post-tax yield you can get is 6 percent. The vast majority of salaried people pay income tax at the 26 percent rate. This means they net 9 percent on their 12 percent savings earnings. In addition, the first $1,000 of investment income in Canada is tax free. Thus, people with less than $8,000 of capital earn their 12 percent tax free.

These high interest rates, of course, may be only temporary, but the important thing to remember is that low interest rates do not upset the term-savings plan. Take as low an interest rate as you will, you cannot work out a plan which will give you a lower return than that sold by the companies. Even if you hide your savings in a mattress and get no interest at all, those savings are not lost but become part of the estate when you die. If you give them to the insurance company, the company takes your savings if you die.

**General Arguments**

Salesmen are ingenious people and, moreover, their sole source of income is the premium they can persuade you to pay. The larger the premium, the better their standard of living. So you will come up against all sorts of arguments in your dealings with them, and it is impossible to put you on your guard against all of them. One thing you can do is look very carefully at all arguments beginning "most people...". Remember that you are not "most people". You are you, and your case is unique. Besides, most arguments which begin with this weak generalization are weak in themselves. They are unverifiable, because you have no way of knowing what "most people" say or do or think.

The best general advice in dealing with the salesman is this:

1. Remember that money earns interest.
2. Then calculate—don't argue.
3. Get the salesman to set down his best proposition in writing and sign it. Then, after he leaves, you can study it at leisure.
4. Don't underestimate the powers of the salesman.

# Chapter 8 Here Is How They Appropriate Your Money

*Prudential paid no surrender
value on policies that lapsed before
the end of three years. Since over
two-thirds of the policy-holders
stopped paying on their policies
within this period, the company
was able to confiscate the reserves
on most of the policies it had written.*
    R. SHULMAN, *The Billion Dollar
    Bookies*, p. 92

### How the Companies Can Do You In

The companies themselves have eleven major ways of increasing their take. These are all carefully hidden by the "no disclosure" policy that is characteristic of the industry.

### 1. Tired old mortality tables

Gollin devotes an entire chapter in his 1966 book *Pay Now, Die Later* to the industry's use of obsolete mortality tables. The mortality tables on which some companies base their premiums were worked out over 100 years ago for the lives of men in a city, where life is notoriously short. In 1858 people were still dying like flies from diseases which are almost extinct today. Since that time the average length of life has increased greatly, and the medical examination screens out bad insurance risks. These factors make a difference in favor of the companies, as Table 22 shows.

It is true that many companies now use later tables of mortality such as the 1941 and 1958 C.S.O. (Commissioners Standard Ordinary) and the $X_{18}$ of the late fifties. But even these are thirty to forty years old. With the development of modern medicare and better

| Age | 20 | 25 | 30 | 35 | 40 | 45 | 50 | 55 | 60 | 65 | 70 |
|---|---|---|---|---|---|---|---|---|---|---|---|
| Number of people per 1,000 expected by the insurance companies to die at this age (American Experience table) | 8 | 8 | 8 | 9 | 10 | 11 | 14 | 19 | 27 | 40 | 62 |
| Number of people per 1,000 actually dying at this age (Dominion Bureau of Statistics figures) | 1 | 1 | 1 | 2 | 3 | 4 | 7 | 11 | 16 | 20 | 26 |

**Table 22.** *The difference between current mortality rates and those used by some companies to determine premiums*

nutrition, people are living longer, and hence we should be paying less for life insurance. Rates are down, but not to an extent commensurate with the increased life spans of the last forty years.

## 2. Super-conservative accounting

The law requires that insurance companies put aside reserves and surplus funds, to make sure no company will go bankrupt and be unable to meet its obligations. But for years the companies have been systematically overestimating needs and overcharging on premiums. James E. Walter of the Harvard Business School finds that legal reserves are 10 percent to 15 percent higher than they need be, surplus funds are maintained at the same levels, and investment income is running 30 percent higher than necessary. Gollin, commenting on this in *Pay Now, Die Later*, says: "Our life insurance companies have evidently accumulated a treasure of $57 billion that will *never* be needed to pay claims and will *never* be returned to us or to our beneficiaries."

This immense pool of money is the result of needless overcharges for service. As a result of the overcharges, millions of families have gone underinsured, and have suffered endless anxiety and hardship.

### 3. Forfeiture of lapsed policies

You are an ordinary salaried worker. A year ago a slick salesman persuaded you to buy "permanent" life insurance at a fancy price. Now you realize that you can't possibly afford the premium and you give it up. This leaves your wife and family without protection, but that is not the worst. This multi-billion-dollar industry, with $57 billion stashed away in unneeded reserves alone, is going to take your savings in the policy. As I have pointed out, *most* of the first premium you paid was not for insurance for that year but for the touted "forced savings" plan. When you cancel in the early years of the policy, you lose everything. In the United States, the best estimate of early-years loss is that 25 percent of all policies are allowed to lapse within thirteen months. So much for "lifetime", "permanent", "peace of mind" and other words predominating in the newspaper ads. This lapse rate costs the ex-policyholders two billion dollars a year in cash, and takes away an estimated ten billion of their protection.

The lapse scandal is hard to pin down in exact figures, but no one doubts its existence. Some investigators (Gollin, Shulman, Epstein, and Gilbert) attribute it to fraud on the part of the companies and the salesmen, and some (Carruthers, McLeod, and Belth) to mere ignorance and incompetence on the part of insurance industry managers, but none of them denies it is a fact. The death claim, which after all is the raison d'être for the whole insurance industry, is a relatively rare way for a policy to terminate. Only 20 percent of U.S. policies (1964 figures) come to this happy end. Most writers on the industry feel that about four out of every five policies end up as lapses or cancellations, or in some other way that fails to fulfill their basic insurance function.

In Canada the situation is even worse. Some students claim that nearly all (90 percent) of insurance policies bought fail in some way to fulfill the job for which they are purchased. Think of your own experience. At one time or another nearly everyone has bought a policy and then given it up within three years. Remember that the average length of time that insurance policies are maintained in force is seven years, according to competent analysts. The value of ordinary life policies surrendered in Canada in 1961 was $612 million. Taking the average amount of insurance to be $1,000, this means that 612,000 Canadians suffered realized losses that year. These ranged from $20 to $6,000 or even higher.

In 1961, policy cessations for the causes shown represented the amounts set out in Table 23 in millions of dollars.

|   | Death | Maturity | Disability | Expiry | Surrender | Lapse |
|---|-------|----------|------------|--------|-----------|-------|
| a | 145.8 | 34.3 | 2.9 | 101.4 | 611.8 | 1,093.4 |
| b | 76.1 | 45.2 | .7 | 106.9 | 275.9 | 516.4 |
| c | 221.9 | 79.4 | 3.6 | 208.3 | 887.7 | 1,609.8 |
|   | 443.8 | 158.9 | 7.2 | 416.6 | 1,775.4 | 3,219.6 |

**Table 23.** *Policy cessations by cause and type (in millions of dollar)*

These figures are taken from the report of the Superintendent of Insurance for Canada. The letters a, b, and c represent ordinary, group, and industrial insurance respectively. The total of non-regular terminations (expiry, surrender, lapse) was $5,411.6 million. Of this, ordinary life made up $1,806.6 million. During 1961, $4,367 million new ordinary insurance was sold. This means that for every $1,000 worth of new insurance bought by careful, cautious Canadians that year, other careful, cautious Canadians lost $413 through irregular terminations. And remember, this was not a depression year, but a good year in the middle of a long boom.

Bringing these figures up to date is not easy because the federal Department of Insurance has changed its system of reporting. In 1982 policy cessations by death amounted to $1,302 million, and cessations by surrender amounted to $1,031 million. The headings "cessations by expiry" and "cessations by lapse" seem to have disappeared, as has the breakdown by type of policy. However, taking the figures available at their face value, it would seem that in 1982 just over 44 percent of policies terminated in surrender.

A better indication of the eventual fate of life-insurance contracts is to be obtained by using figures provided under oath at investigations in the U.S. Congress. Belth, testifying at hearings by the late Senator Philip A. Hart on life-insurance abuses, said that in his opinion the 13-month lapse rate was 40 percent, and that his study of fifty-nine large U.S. companies indicated that, by the end of the tenth year, 47 percent of ordinary life policies had been discontinued (Source: Spielman & Zelman, p. 150).

Three simple examples are shown in Table 24.

| | Total amount of premiums paid | Cost of equivalent term insurance | Net loss |
|---|---|---|---|
| Chris Cretin bought a life policy, premium to age 65, in 1935 when he was 48. He paid quarterly a yearly premium of $580 for a $10,000 policy. After 2 years he found he had been talked into something he couldn't afford, and stopped paying premiums. His losses: | $1160 | $250 | $910 |
| Caspar Milquetoast bought an ordinary life policy for $1,000 at age 35. The premium was $24.59. One year later he gave it up. His losses: | $24.59 | $7.75 | $16.84 |
| Gordon Gruel bought a 10-year endowment for $10,000 "with profits" at a cost of $990.80 at age 40. Two years later he gave it up. His losses: | $1,981.60 | $181.60 | $1,800 |

**Table 24.** *The results of typical "early-years loss"*

## 4. Optimistic "dividend" projections that turned out to be false

How many of these lapsed policies were bought because the sales-man assured the buyer that the annual premiums would be much reduced by the payment of "dividends"? How often did he forget to say that dividend payments don't begin until after the third policy year? By this time it is often too late. Never buy a policy solely because the dividend history of the company is good and the dividends high. The exotic way the insurance companies use the word "dividend" requires some explanation.

Normally, a dividend is a distribution to shareholders of a portion of a corporation's post-tax profits. But in life-insurance usage, as I have mentioned, a dividend is a partial return of overcharges. If in paying the original premium you have been overcharged a great deal, the resulting dividend may be quite large. But remember that you are not sharing in earnings; what you are receiving is a small part of your own money that you overpaid in premiums three or four years before.

Even this definition leans over backwards in being fair to the insurance companies. Actually, in many policies you never get a cent of your overcharges back. What the companies are returning to you under the name of "dividends" is the *interest* earned by your overpayments after all the costs of insurance and of doing business are paid.

Consider this 20-pay life policy, taken out at age 25 (Table 25). At this age, the death rate for Canadian males is 1.48 per thousand. Therefore the cost of insuring one of each thousand insured men, sick or well, for $10,000 for one year is $15. This company charges $264.

From Table 25 you can see that, in the early years at least, the dividends are merely a partial return of the *interest* earned by your overpayments. The overpayments themselves are kept by the company. At the end of the third year most policies begin to have a cash surrender value. In our example, this amounts to 42 percent of the accumulated overcharges and interest.

Since all companies use dividends as a selling point, they tend to overestimate the amount which is likely to be paid in a given period. The actual record of dividends paid almost invariably shows that the estimates made by the company were high. But even using the optimistic estimates made by the company, they turn out to be merely partial returns of the interest earned by your overcharges, or, at best, returns of a small part of the overcharges themselves.

| Years held | Premium | Actual Cost of insurance | Overcharge | Interest on overcharge for year at 5% | Interest compounded to date | "Dividend" paid by company | Cash surrender value |
|---|---|---|---|---|---|---|---|
| 1 | $264 | $15 | $249 | $12 | $12 | $ 0 | $ 0 |
| 2 | 264 | 15 | 249 | 12 | 25 | 8 | 0 |
| 3 | 264 | 15 | 249 | 12 | 38 | 10 | 330 |

**Table 25.** *The relationship between "dividends" and the interest on overcharges. 1963 rates are used so that dividends can be traced exactly.*

Some salesmen who have a low opinion of your intelligence may tell you that dividends are the interest on the money you have entrusted to the company. The company has put this to work earning for you, and pays you the proceeds each year. The way to demolish this argument is to ask what money of yours the company has in its possession. This turns out to consist of:

1. The overcharges made by the company when figuring your premium.
2. The accumulated cash surrender value of your policy.

If the dividends are a return of the interest earned by your cash value, then when you borrow on your policy to the full extent of this amount, the dividends must stop because the principal is gone. But they do not stop; therefore, the only other source of dividends, the overcharges made in the premium, must be the one used.

### 5. Death benefits refused

Even if you try to collect from the insurance company by going to the extreme of dying, they have ways and means of avoiding payment. Most people know nothing of the number of disputed claims which reach the courts each year. In the period from 1929 to 1961, there were at least 387 reported decisions handed down in Canadian life-insurance legal cases—an average of twelve a year. The companies have well-paid lawyers, and can afford to go to court better than can your widow. So for every case that reaches the stage of a public hearing in the courts, there must be hundreds that are settled by the bewildered beneficiary out of court, and on the insurance company's terms.

This is a nasty thing for me to say, and I'm sorry it has to be said. But I put it forth with some confidence because of my experiences on "phone-in" radio and television programs in cities across Canada in 1982 and 1983. A surprising number of callers had problems that had to do with collecting death or disability benefits from life-insurance companies. In addition to collecting court records, I am also, as a public service, making a card file of cases that have not yet reached the courts. Some of these come from newspaper ombudsman files. But the best source is the victim himself. If you, dear reader, have such a case, let me know the details. I don't promise I can do anything, but I do agree not to use the material without written permission from you, your heirs, or assigns.

### 6. Avoiding communication. The fine print; incomprehensible language; pious gobbledegook

When you have something to hide, it is best to use a foreign language and hide it away at the bottom of the page in minuscule print. The life-insurance industry has mastered all these tricks to the point where they think it is *normal* to communicate with the public this way. In the mid-seventies, the then president of the Canadian Life Insurance Association said that a life-insurance policy is a legal contract and *therefore* cannot be expressed in clear language (emphasis mine). Carruthers, quoting this with characteristic mildness in his 1975 Royal Commission Report, says merely that it is "absurd". I would go farther. I always thought it was the lawyers' *job* to write contracts in a form that both parties could understand.

Whatever the source of confusion, the vast majority of life-insurance buyers don't know what they are buying. I say this is mostly the fault of the industry and its salesmen.

### 7. Expense ratios

All insurance companies waste their policyholders' money, but some waste more of it than others. A company's total admitted costs divided by the total amount of insurance it sells is called its "expense ratio". Companies which have low ratios either are operating on a less regal scale, or else have hit upon a more efficient way to hide disbursements. The expense ratios for some well-known companies are shown in Table 26.

| Company | According to: | | |
| | Stone & Cox | Berman | Prudential of England |
|---|---|---|---|
| Canadian Life | 12% | | 19% |
| Continental Life | 14 | | |
| T. Eaton Life | 9 | | |
| Great Western Life | 9 | | 21 |
| Imperial Life | 13 | | |
| London Life | 11 | | 23 |
| Manufacturers Life | 9 | | |
| Metropolitan Life | 9 | 14 | 17 |
| Mutual of Canada | 10 | | 18 |
| New York Life | 8 | 12 | |
| Prudential of England | 7 | | 12 |
| Prudential of America | 7 | 15 | |
| Sun Life | 9 | | 28 |

**Table 26.** *Expense ratios of some insurance companies (all about 1960)*

All of these "cost-of-doing-business" figures must be taken with a grain of salt because of their source. Every company wants to put out numbers proving that it is better than its competitors. Stone & Cox does not want to offend any of its customers, i.e. the insurance companies. But you don't have to be a detective to see that the cost of doing business in the insurance industry is very high. Palatial offices in downtown marble halls, extravagant executive salaries, multi-million-dollar sales conventions, in-house, four-color magazines, trips to the Caribbean for sales-contest winners, full-page ads in newspapers and magazines, TV spots—they all add up. People who know the industry, such as Carruthers, Gollin, and Shulman, make much of the sheer inefficiency of its management cadres, and it is hard to quarrel with this judgement. They have so much money that over decades of automatic growth and easy living they have gone soft. Even the automobile industry, never noted for the brainpower of its executives, looks good compared with the vacillating top executives of life insurance.

## 8. The agency system

Direct sale by the insurance company to the individual is the most wasteful, expensive, and old-fashioned sales system in existence. So, of course, this is the system used almost universally in the life-insurance business. To recruit and partly control the salesmen, you need an agency and one or more agency managers, so you build up overhead expenses more and more. A hundred years ago some autocratic boss intoned: "Life insurance is not bought, it has to be *sold*," and no one in the industry has bothered to examine the proposition since.

Marketing, as an art and a science, has made tremendous progress since the nineteenth century, but you wouldn't know it by looking at insurance advertising and marketing practices. In many ways insurance is the most backward industry of all; in marketing, communications, management—you name it—it is even worse than the government.

## 9. Unfair underwriting

The actuaries who work out the cost of insuring various types and ages of people are supposed to be well-educated professionals, and usually they are. But the trouble is, they have little influence over the top executives who set company policy. This leads to some scandalous underwriting.

For example, it has been known for generations that women live longer than men, yet it is only in the last decade that it has become possible for women to pay lower premiums than men. The case is self-evident: the average woman survives to age 76, the average man to age 72. Since she has four more years to pay premiums, before she needs the services of the industry, each premium should be less.

Another case of unfair underwriting is the cigarette scandal. It has been known for forty years that smoking shortens life, and for ten years even the U.S. government has noticed it, and forced cigarette advertisers to say: "Warning: the surgeon general has determined that cigarette smoking is dangerous to your health." This should be clear enough, even for a life-insurance executive. But most companies still charge everyone the same age, cigarette smoker or not, the same premium.

### 10. Unfair pressure on borrowers from the investment department

It is a matter of opinion (and there is room for a wide diversity of opinion) what percentage of a life-insurance company's assets should be in common stocks or equities. The law has taken the view that some limit should be enforced, and there is a degree of consensus around 10 percent. But the way things are, depending on what point he is trying to make, an insurance man can say that his company has 3 percent of its assets in equities, or it has 30 percent in equities. Thus he has it both ways. If he wants his company to look solid and conservative, he uses the 3 percent figure; if he wants to project an image of modern competitive business, he uses the 30 percent figure.

The difference in the percentages quoted by the insurance man is caused by including the sweeteners (equity, warrants, conversion privileges, etc.) that his investment department is able to squeeze out of borrowing companies, because they have so much money to lend. If the company wants the loan, it must be prepared to give up some of its common stock.

According to the *Life Insurance Fact Book, 1981* (p. 74), the industry has lent privately to corporations some $80 billion. Of this, an estimated $70 billion was arranged by direct negotiation. As Gollin points out in *Pay Now, Die Later* (p. 145), speaking of the smaller but still substantial numbers of the late sixties: "That is, six-sevenths of this immense corporate indebtedness [to the life-insurance industry] is money that has changed hands privately, in deals kept secret from outsiders."

### 11. Gimmick policies

What is really needed in the life-insurance industry is *simplification*. This should apply to policies, prices, propaganda, and personnel. The response of the industry to this need is typical: it is making insurance more and more complicated.

A good example is minimum-deposit insurance. In the U.S. you are allowed to deduct from taxable income the interest you have paid on loans to buy life insurance. Many companies have now come out with schemes under which you borrow all or most of the money needed to pay the premium, secured by the cash value of the policy itself. In the early years you have your protection and some tax shelter, and all seems well. But very soon the accumulated borrowing mounts up, premium rates rise, and you find yourself with very little death protection. I am glad to see that the Internal Revenue Service has recently vetoed this scheme, but other gimmick policies will take its place. So long as the industry is competing frantically to place policies rather than do a public service, schemes like this will exist. They make money for the company, but do nothing but harm to the individual.

## How the Salesman Can Do a Job on You

Just as the company has eleven ways of making you pay extra for protection, the man on the front line, the salesman, has his own eleven ways of doing you in.

### 1. Rebating (refunding some of the premiums as an inducement to buy)

This is very common, but it is against the law. If the salesman offers you a rebate, he is a crook. Don't deal with a crook. You could both land up in jail.

### 2. Misrepresentation of "dividends" paid in the past

This is sometimes (but seldom) done in published form by the companies, but most often it is an informal sales gimmick of the salesman himself. Consumers' Union says, in *Life Insurance* (p. 92): "Questionable dividend practices are also of concern because they may distort the price comparisons made by current buyers. By raising dividends on recent business only (which costs the company relatively little), a company can develop attractive dividend scales for sales illustrations that may make the company look better in cost comparisons than it deserves to." It is hard to verify, so watch out. The simple way to avoid this particular scam is to have a rule: never buy a participating policy.

### 3. Quoting low prices to get the business

When the policy is delivered, the salesman explains that he made a "mistake". Make him take it back. Salesmen make enough inadvertent mistakes without your having to pay for those he made on purpose.

### 4. Selling the high-commission types of insurance

All you have to do is remember who is paying.

### 5. Poor training

The huge sums expended on training a salesman are spent teaching him to *sell*, not to know about the services his company can provide. Besides, by next year, when you want to ask him a question, he will probably be in another line of business. The answer to the question "Who fixes stupidly, incompetently, or dishonestly arranged life insurance?" is "Nobody". Remember that the salesman is not a trusted planner of your estate, but a huckster who makes his living by selling high-premium types of insurance. The type of policy which is best for the salesman and the company is the worst possible type for you. Remember that the average salesman is a smooth operator and no fool. Do not underestimate his powers. The best way to hold your own with him is to know in advance what he is going to say. If you know his arguments against term insurance in advance, then it can be quite fun to hear him recite them one by one.

### 6. Exaggerated cash-value figures

You shouldn't be buying a policy with "cash values" anyway, but to the extent the salesman thinks this is important to you, he will be tempted to quote false figures. They are not easy to check with many policies, even when you have the actual contract in hand. And by that time, of course, you have paid out your money. The "cash surrender value" or "savings portion" of an insurance policy has nothing whatsoever to do with the policy itself. It is a selling point used to confuse those who do not know that money earns interest. The "cash value" is meaningless unless you give up your insurance protection, and is forfeited to the company if you die. For these reasons the "cash value" of a policy is neither "investment" nor "savings" in any sense of these words.

### 7. Switching

The salesman is adept at "trading you up" to a more expensive, less-protective, or better-commission-generating policy. He is just like the furniture salesman who will fill your living room with cheap and tasteless furniture, but there is a difference: the furniture will fall apart after a year or so, but a badly chosen insurance policy will cost you dearly until you are lucky enough to die.

## 8. Selling a related service

If your salesman sells mutual funds, or money funds, or real estate, and offers to get you a bargain in one of these areas, show him the door. Most insurance salesmen don't know enough about their own business to make themselves of any use to you. Why should they be offering services in related areas where they know even less?

## 9. Hidden bribes or favors

This is another approach to rebating, but harder to prove. Nevertheless, if you are found out, you may both go to jail.

## 10. Concealment of extra charges

The deal is made, you have signed the application for insurance and given the salesman a check. His commission is in the bag. But his underwriting department decides that, because of your health or your occupation, you must pay a higher rate. The salesman is sometimes tempted to keep this bad news from you, even paying the difference in premiums himself. You find out the correct premium *next* year, when the bill arrives at your home, and the salesman has moved on to something else.

## 11. Twisting

There are two kinds of twisting, both involving the cancellation of an older policy. The first kind is when the insurance salesman helps you to cancel your old "cash value" policy so you will have money enough to pay his commission on the new super-duper executive policy he is about to sell you. Whether or not a shift from one "cash value" policy to another is to your advantage depends on the two policies. There are tremendous differences in price between ordinary life policies from different companies. If you make your price comparisons properly, using Belth, or Consumers' Union (see Bibliography), you might well save money in the twist. But don't trust a salesman to make the calculations for you.

The second kind of twisting is that mentioned at other places in the book, when you cancel a "cash value" policy and buy term insurance. The salesman is not likely to bother you with this kind of twisting, because the term commission is small.

The basic fact you should know when considering twisting is: the salesman is *not* on your side. Ben Feldman, a New York Life salesman who once held the record for sales to individuals, says, in *Newsweek* (Oct. 19, 1964, p. 86): "I try to make the customer uncomfortable, very uncomfortable. When a man says no, I don't hear him." In Toronto, salesmen have been known to put toy paper coffins on your desk, while enlarging on the horrors to be visited on your dependants after your untimely death. This may be despised as kiddie stuff, but watch out. These techniques have been tested at huge expense on thousands of victims, and have proved themselves in selling the high-cost/low-protection types of insurance. Salvatore Giordano, a Prudential salesman in New York, says, also in *Newsweek* (Oct. 19, 1964, p. 86): "The training manuals tell you to put the prospect's head right through the windshield and make him watch the blood drip."

# Chapter 9 The Savings Plan

*Savings through life insurance*
*may be hazardous to your wealth.*
     ROBERT I. MEHR, Editor, *Jour-*
     *nal of Risk and Insurance*, 1979, in
     J. Alex Murray, ed., *Insuring North*
     *Americans*, p. 215

My advice that you should buy term insurance exclusively does not depend on what you decide to do with the money you save. It stands on its merits, namely that you buy maximum protection for your dependants during the period when you provide their sole financial support.

Your choice of the right kind of term insurance to protect your dependants will result (if you are already insured) in your finding money in your hip pocket. A large sum may come back to you in the form of cash-surrender value of the old policy. In addition, each year you will save the difference between the low premiums for term insurance and the high premiums for "cash value" insurance. This money is yours to spend any way you wish. If you think it wise to spend it to enrich your family life by travel, education, or other means, no one can prove you wrong.

However, the conventional way to think about your cash savings, both the lump sum at the beginning and the annual savings on premiums, is to say that you are responsible for the well-being of another dependant, namely yourself, and you should have a system of regular savings for him or her. You save money in order to have security. By this you mean that, if something unforeseen happens and you cease to have a regular income, you will be able to get along on your investments and savings. This something unforeseen may happen tomorrow, but it is more likely to happen when you are old and unable to compete in the labor market. The money you put aside to protect you in this eventuality should be divided into three portions, and put into three different kinds of savings. But before you do this, consider what the characteristics of a good investment should be.

## The Yield of Investments

Money left to its own devices in a bank term deposit, etc., earns interest, and grows larger in amount each year. The rate at which your money grows is called the interest rate. If you have religious or other scruples against taking money that you have done nothing to earn, you can bury your cash in a deep well, and when you take it out you will find that the dollar amount is exactly the same as when it was put in. But if you take your money to the Shattered Trust Company or any investment house, they will "put it to work" for you, and your investment is certain either to increase or decrease each year. Whether your money grows or shrinks depends in most cases on the part of the business cycle we are traversing.

There is only one kind of investment that yields a negative rate of interest in good times and bad. This is the ordinary life-insurance policy in its early years. Any investment from which you take out less money than you put in has a negative rate of interest. If you give up the ordinary insurance policy within ten years—and, as I've said, the average life of all policies is seven years—you get back less than you have put in. (This is true even after subtracting the cost of insuring you. Since pure insurance is a service, once it is rendered there can be no refund.)

The yield on life-insurance policies as an investment is from minus 20 percent to 0 percent in the earlier years. Therefore, if you want your money to earn interest, and are looking for a place to invest it, a life-insurance policy is the worst possible place to do it.

For example, here is a "low rate" ordinary-life policy taken out at age 24. The amount is $5,000 and the annual premium $62.39. Consider the situation at the fifth year. The insured has obtained for his premiums two things: $5,000 worth of term insurance and a certain amount of "savings". The average annual cost of renewable term over the 5-year period, when taken out at age 24, is $1.73 a thousand. Therefore, the cost of the insurance part is $8.64 a year ($1.73 x 5), and the rest of the premium ($53.75) must be considered savings. So, under this policy, we have "saved" $53.75 a year for five years, or $268.75. Now let's see how much we can get out by giving up the protection. (Of course, if you are not willing to give up the protection, you get nothing.) The cash value of this policy at the fifth year (including accumulated dividends) is $191.25. Now, if a sum of $53.75 is paid annually into an investment giving *minus* 16 percent compounded annually, the amount of the investment at the end of five years is $191.06. Therefore, *minus* 16 percent is the rate at which your "savings" are earning money.

The average miser has a better investment system than this. He puts his yearly savings into a mattress. At the end of five years he gets back all the money he put in. This is an interest rate of 0 percent, which is a princely yield compared to that of the insurance policy.

From the point of view of earning power, or yield, the conventional investments during boom times stack up about like this, beginning with the worst possible investment and working up to the best:

| | |
|---|---|
| Life insurance | Minus 20 percent to 0 percent in the early years; plus 0 percent to 4 percent after 10 to 40 years |
| Savings banks | plus 6 percent to 8 percent |
| Government bonds | plus 8 percent to 12 percent |
| Industrial stocks | plus 4 percent to 10 percent |
| Real estate | plus 5 percent to 20 percent |
| Average successful small business | plus 10 percent to 30 percent |

## Safety of the Principal

But in addition to earning power, there are two other factors which should be considered in choosing an investment. These are safety of the principal, and availability. No matter how high an interest rate your money earns in the first year, if the principal disappears in the second, your books will show a loss.

## Safety of Dollars

There are two ways you can lose the principal: actual loss of dollars, and loss of purchasing power. Since all businesses and financial institutions depend for their stability on the government, the safest possible dollar investment is a government bond. If the government repudiated its bonds, all insurance companies, all banks, all investment houses, and most businesses would be bankrupt overnight, because their assets are for the most part tied up in government securities. The next-safest place for your money is probably a savings bank, and after this point it is difficult to assign any order to the various investments from the point of view of safety. Gold mines sometimes fail to find gold, and oil wells are drilled without touching oil. Scores of life-insurance companies have gone bankrupt in the past, and there is no reason to think that more will not fail in the future. Imagine what would happen if a new resistant form of flu turned out to be the Black Death coming back in disguise. One-third of the population of Europe was wiped out by the Black Death over a ten-year period. Are you *sure* that nothing like this can happen again? Remember that a real epidemic can drive an insurance company to the wall. Therefore, from the point of view of safety, a life-insurance policy is certainly not the best, and may be among the worst, of investments.

### Safety of Purchasing Power

Economists agree that the purchasing power of the dollar has been dropping for forty years. You don't have to be trained in economics or other occult subjects to realize this. Just think back and compare what you used to pay for food, clothing, rent, and cars with what you pay today. This is called inflation. There is some debate among economists about how fast the dollar is losing its purchasing power, but a conservative rate is 5 percent a year. This means that an insurance policy paid off at its full face value in dollars after twenty-three years will have lost exactly two-thirds of its purchasing power. You have put in $1 dollars and you take out 33¢ dollars.

This is the one sense in which the insurance companies' use of the word "guaranteed" is correct. As much as anything can be guaranteed in this uncertain world, life-insurance "savings" are guaranteed money-losers. When the life companies use *your* money to advertise that "savings in a life insurance policy are guaranteed", they are promising you that the dollars you take out will almost certainly buy less than the dollars you put in.

### Availability

From the point of view of availability, savings are of three kinds:

1. Liquid assets, such as bank accounts, and stocks and bonds which can be sold on short notice.

2. Contingent, or hypothetical, assets—the money you can borrow from the bank at 12 percent interest if you mortgage your house; or from a loan company for a lien on your car; or from a pawnshop for a lien on your coat or your camera. With most conventional insurance policies you are allowed to borrow (at 6 percent to 8 percent) a certain percentage of the cash value of the policy. This is borrowing from your heirs, but nevertheless it must be considered a hypothetical asset.

3. Frozen assets. Your contribution to a retirement fund which will pay you $500 a month at age 65 is a frozen asset until you reach 65 and the payments begin. An annuity is this sort of asset.

Each type of savings has its advantages and disadvantages. Liquid assets are wonderfully easy to withdraw and spend. This is sometimes an advantage, and sometimes not. If you lose a lawsuit, they can be taken away from you by court order, but on the other hand if you are suddenly forced to go to hospital for six months, liquid assets are useful.

Contingent assets are not so easy to realize in cash, and this again is sometimes good and sometimes bad. If a sharper persuades you to invest in his own peculiar brand of gold brick, the fact that it takes several days to get the cash gives you time to think it over, and may save your money. On the other hand, if the law suddenly catches up with you, and you are arrested and want to get out on bail, you cannot leave a car or an insurance policy as security and be a free man; you must have cash.

Frozen assets are best for security, worst for availability. Money sunk into a company pension plan is stuck there until you reach the retirement age, and is then paid out to you in monthly installments as long as you live. Money that cannot be touched by court order, bankruptcy proceedings, or an over-optimistic investor can be a wonderful comfort. If you kill someone with your car, and lose the resulting damage suit, a court order can strip you of everything you own, and can garnishee your wages for years to come. But it cannot touch the principal of a pension.

Each of these three types of savings has its own peculiar merits and uses, and therefore it is wise if possible to spread your savings to encompass a little of each type. Keep some money in the bank to tide you over sudden emergencies. Make some payments on a home; your equity in it is a form of savings, and you will find it useful if you need to borrow money for a more serious emergency. Finally, put something into a pension plan, in order to have one kind of savings which both you and your investment counsellors are powerless to destroy.

## Choose Some Savings That Hedge Against Inflation

Nobody knows what the value of the dollar is going to be twenty years from now, but most indicators point to its being less than it is today. Pensioners, widows, and genteel annuitants, the people most hurt by inflation, have relatively little political power. On the other hand, trade unions, speculators, property-owners, civil servants, and professional men have great political power, and can defend themselves from inflation by raising their prices. This is one reason why many people think the inflationary trend will continue. Another powerful factor is the high level of government debt. If you were deeply in debt, wouldn't you be tempted to hope for inflation, so that your debts could be paid off in 50-cent dollars?

At the price of slightly increased risk, you can have a reasonable yield, plus some hedge against inflation, if you put the savings portion of your plan into equity-type investments. These include real estate, mutual funds, a portfolio of diversified stocks, and convertible bonds. For a detailed discussion of the advantages and disadvantages of the various types of investments, see my *Start with $1000: Do-It-Yourself Investing for Canadians,* Macmillan of Canada, 1982.

If you are not troubled by scruples, perhaps the best equity investment you can find, combining the virtues of safety, liquidity, good yield, and rapid capital growth, is the stock of life-insurance companies. Scruples are a highly personal affair. Some people won't invest in liquor stocks, or become a part-owner of a brothel, because they feel the product is harmful socially, or is in some way a racket. The life-insurance business is undoubtedly a legal racket, but it is accepted as a respectable part of our society, and there is no reason why an honest man can't invest in the business until such time as society decides against it. I can't invest in life-insurance stocks, because I feel it would be inconsistent or worse for me to be writing about the evil machinations of the life companies while at the same time enjoying the profits that come from their exploitation of the consumer. But I wish I could. If, in 1943, when I first began to study the life-insurance industry, I had invested in $1,000 worth of Lincoln

National Insurance stock, the holding would be worth $139,000 today. In addition, I would be getting $1,000 a year in dividends!

This is the answer you give to your insurance salesman if he claims the term-savings plan will fail because you don't know how to invest, and will lose the savings portion in some mad scheme. You tell him you are going to put all your savings portion each year into insurance-company stock. Then you have him up a tree either way. If he says the stock is no good, he is undermining his own industry; if he says the stock is a fine investment, he is endorsing your term-savings plan!

How to meet inflation is the most serious problem facing the investor today. This is particularly true if you are young or middle-aged. If you are nearly ready to retire, it is almost too late to worry, because you have already lost most of the purchasing power of your early savings.

All the ways of saving outlined above have their advantages and disadvantages.

But never, under any circumstances, should you put your money into an insurance policy as an investment. From every point of view, life insurance as an investment is ideally bad. Here is a checklist of what's bad about life insurance as an investment:

## 1. Yield

In the early years, life insurance gives the worst return known to man, always returning less money than you have put in. This happens even in boom times when all other forms of investment are yielding plus rates of interest. In the later years, life insurance can, under some policies, yield as high as 4 percent, but this is rare, and you have to wait many years to collect.

## 2. Safety

Life insurance is tied to our business economy, and is therefore no safer than the recurring cycles of boom and depression allow. In addition, the solvency of a life company is always dependent on the control of epidemic diseases. If they get out of control, you lose both your investment and your protection. Finally, if you do collect, it is almost certain that the dollars you get will have greatly diminished buying power.

### 3. Unavailability

Life-insurance investments are about as unavailable as it is possible to be. You can't withdraw your savings in the early years at all. In the later years you can clearly get a loan of your own money but must pay the company 6 percent to 8 percent for the privilege. The only way you can cleanly get any part of your money out of your investment is by giving up your insurance protection.

### 4. Confiscation

Added to all these disadvantages is one crowning touch. If you die, you lose every cent of your savings in the insurance policy! The company pays the face value of the insurance to your estate, but keeps all your savings for itself.

### The Problem of Commissions

When you go to a banker, insurance salesman, or stockbroker to buy a financial service, you are subject to nameless fears. This is not surprising, because your common sense tells you that the seller knows more about financial services than you do. Thus, there is a good chance of your being taken for a ride.

The largest sums you spend each year are handed over to financial people. Time-payment plans, mortgage payments, personal-loan installments, and life-insurance premiums eat up the bulk of most people's income. Yet it is in the area of financial buying that people are least informed. Many men know how to choose a good used car, and many housewives are shrewd buyers of meat. But almost nobody knows how to get the greatest value for each dollar when buying financial services.

One reason why financial services are harder to buy than consumer goods is the method of paying the salesman. The job of selling most financial services is paid for by commissions, and the commission is based on the total amount of money you pay. Thus, the seller of any financial service, if he is to live, has to sell you the most expensive service whether or not it fits your needs. Life-insurance salesmen get 60 percent to 100 percent of the premium you pay in the first year, and 5 percent of the premium for the next nine years. Personal loan companies get from 18 percent to 30 percent on the money you borrow. Hence, if it turns out upon examination that you really don't *need* a personal loan, you can't expect the loan officer to tell you. It would be money out of his pocket. Stockbrokers get about ½ of 1 percent of the price of any stocks you buy, and the same commission when you sell. Reputable stockbrokers do not switch their clients from one stock to another without reason. Yet it is difficult to blame a broker for wanting to buy and sell for his clients, since that is the only way he gets paid. The mutual-fund salesman gets from 5 percent to 9 percent of the money you pay for your savings plan, and in addition you have to pay indirectly all the buying and selling commissions of the brokers he hires.

Not many people would be so bold as to claim the financial world could be organized any other way. The commission method of selling does get things sold, and some of the financial services sold are of genuine benefit to consumers. But on the other hand, since the salesman's living expenses are to be paid with your money, you have to be especially careful when buying any kind of financial service.

## Annuities

In the old days, when a dollar was a dollar, the annuity was a simple and popular way of providing income after retirement. You paid so much a year until retirement date, then the annuity paid you so much a year until you died. Double-digit inflation made a shambles of annuity programs in the seventies, and even today, with the rate close to 6 percent, there are much better ways of providing for your old age.

However, many people like the certainty of the dollar return from an annuity. For these people I have only one suggestion: buy your annuity anywhere but from a life-insurance company. Banks, trust companies, and other financial institutions are much more likely to make a full price disclosure. The simplest way to proceed is to go to a financial broker who has access to annuities offered by many sources.

This advice is no good in Canada, where the insurance companies have lobbied their way into a monopoly position. They are the only people licensed to sell life annuities. For a detailed discussion of the problems of collapsing an R.R.S.P. into an annuity between ages 65 and the statutory age of 71, see McLeod, p. 189 (see Bibliography).

# PART III. Know Your Enemy

# Chapter 10 What's a Nice Guy Like You Doing Linked Up with These Awful People?

*The Achilles' heel of the industry is the cost of the agency distribution system, which reflects high costs to the policyholder, the high cost of agency turnover, of lapses, and of policy switching.*
　　MICHAEL P. WALSH, President, 1975, Home Life Insurance Company, quoted in Carruthers, vol.I

## A Little History

I got started thinking about life insurance in exactly the same way every young man gets started. In the small university community of Cornell, where I lived, it was easy to see that my wife was pregnant. So I began to get numerous calls from salesmen wanting to sell me insurance. I listened to what they had to say, and was instantly struck by the wide difference in prices quoted for the same level of protection. I had recently been teaching the binomial theorem to little kids, so I was familiar with how money, left to its own devices, earns interest.

So I began asking questions. The salesmen immediately roused my suspicion by the way they back-pedalled around simple questions such as "How much does it cost?" Cornell had a good library, so I began reading books and magazine articles, and thus opened up the 200-year story of murder, theft, fraud, chicanery, and repeated public investigations that is the history of the industry.

But this did not stop me from buying insurance. Life insurance is a necessity for a young father, particularly one who is not skilled in making money. In those days I was interested in other things. In 1944, when I was 28, I made a choice between a 20-pay life policy of the Prudential of England and my own term-savings plan using Metropolitan 10-year renewable term, a government annuity, and a separate savings fund. Both policies were participating, and the total premium for each of the alternatives (insurance *plus* savings) came to the same figure—$377 a year. I decided on the term-savings plan.

Over the first 10-year period the term insurance cost me $5.80 a thousand, and over the 20-year period ending in 1963, the average cost was $6.09 a thousand. Since during this period I averaged about $15,000 term insurance, my yearly cost averaged about $90. For the first couple of years I put most of the balance ($377 less $90) as savings into a government annuity, but then I began more and more to fear inflation, so I stopped payments on the annuity, and put the savings portion into stocks and real estate.

Within 10 years I was self-insured. That is, if I had wanted to I could have dropped all the term insurance, and my heirs would have been protected by the savings alone. By this time the savings had grown to an amount higher than the face value of the original insurance. Actually, with higher standards of living, I took out more insurance—this time decreasing term from Occidental—and, being somewhat encouraged, pushed the savings plan along even faster.

Using the methods described in this book and in my book on investing called *Start with $1000*, I have doubled my net worth every two years since 1942. Of course, I was a college teacher in those days, so I started with my head under water. Then, too, I don't know how much longer I can keep this up, since doubling gets tougher with each two-year period. Nevertheless, I have demonstrated to my own satisfaction that the term-savings plan works, with no ifs, ands, or buts. And don't think that this result is in any way connected with my being a large earner, because I'm not. I'm good at managing money, not at making it.

### The Book Nobody Wanted

In February 1945 I published the first of two articles in the *Canadian Forum*, suggesting that the government should put an end to this long history of fraud and theft by simply taking over the industry and selling life insurance to everybody at its own experienced mortality rates. Since I was by then working for a large corporation, I prudently published under the pseudonym of "Boris Sherashevski". The articles generated charges and counter-charges, some fairly severe in tone. So I was encouraged by the interest, and wrote a carefully researched book on life insurance. The book was finished late in 1945. It made the rounds of publishers in Canada, the United States, and England. Most publishers said they found the book highly amusing and informative, and they were really sorry they couldn't publish it. Some publishers' readers, after they had finished laughing, went out and made radical changes in their insurance programs. But, nevertheless, they claimed that most people were not willing to spend the time required to read this book. Others felt that the Canadian market was too small, the American market too large, and the English market too different to justify the publication of a book of this nature.

I remember sitting freezing in my 1932 Plymouth convertible, parked on Bond Street in Toronto, outside the editorial offices of Macmillan of Canada, completely paralyzed. I was unable to muster the courage to try the battered manuscript on one more house.

So, after trying publishers for a few years, I gave up. I did this not only because I was discouraged, but because at the back of my mind there was a gnawing uncertainty about the plan itself. In my work as an independent financial consultant, time after time clients would say to me, "Look, I like your plan and it sounds perfectly reasonable to me and I can't see any flaws in it. But, on the other hand, I don't know you, and I do know the life-insurance companies have been respectable members of the business community for a hundred years. What you say runs counter to everything they have been saying for generations. Why should I trust you rather than them?"

There is just enough logic in this query to make it disturbing. "What," I asked myself, "if there is a basic flaw in my insurance-and-savings scheme? What if it looks all right in theory, yet when it is put into practice over a period of years, some fundamental difficulty appears? If through the premature publication of a book I have led hundreds or even thousands of people into a financial trap, it will be on my conscience for the rest of my days."

This slight uncertainty (which has long since been laid to rest) was brought to a head as soon as I began to have clients as a life-insurance consultant.

In Montreal in the early fifties the life-insurance people made a few attempts to put me out of business. But they came to nothing. Once, in a meeting in his office, J. Milton Brown, head of the London Life Agency, said with a great show of confidence that it was illegal for anyone at all to give the advice I give about life insurance, namely to separate the savings and insurance aspects into two different contracts. My client, H. G. Cochrane of Power Corporation, was with us. I had my lawyers send Mr. Brown a letter asking him to put his remarks in writing. There was neither acknowledgement nor reply.

All during the 1950s, in my spare time from making a living, bringing up three sons, and writing other books, I worked at various schemes for getting people to see life insurance my way. I wrote two books larded with the marvellous cartoons of Peter Whalley, whose pictorial genius made the learning process as painless as it could be. I tried jokes. I wrote a farcical *Fortune*-style piece on Todd Morden (whose names suggest "death" in the common western languages), who had become an instant tycoon by using insurance-company techniques to sell death insurance. I even tried radio plays with Michael Sheldon and television cartoon shows with George Feyer. I tried to sell the newspaper syndicates on short pieces of consumer advice, with or without cartoons, saying the opposite to what the insurance companies were saying in the full-page ads.

But nothing worked. I couldn't get any of these bright schemes past the editorial offices, even of those industries not enjoying advertising revenue from the life companies. Faced with this overwhelming evidence that I was not persuasive, I should have dropped everything and concentrated on developing the needed polemical skills. But in those days I still believed that the facts alone were enough to do the job, and in fact I tended to have a low opinion of people who were merely persuasive. So I continued to gather facts and try novel methods of presenting them, but without success.

Finally, rather late in the 1950s, Eugene Holman of the CBC agreed to present a three-part series of radio plays on personal finance. The first was on life insurance. I had made a special effort to be diplomatic in the presentation—no rude words, no suggestion of fraud or chicane—but to no avail. After the play, the CBC telephone circuit boards lighted up like a Christmas tree, and seven hundred transcripts of the program were sent out to listeners before someone higher in the CBC hierarchy thought it would be wise to stop the distribution of seditious material.

At that time I eked out a living as a speech-writer for Alcan Aluminum in Montreal. The day after the CBC program, the president, R. E. Powell, called me into his office for a chewing out. He said he had been called by "several" insurance-company presidents and accused of harboring a Communist on his staff. They wanted me fired, and he (old Rip was not a man to be trifled with) made it clear that if I didn't cease and desist, they would immediately have their desire.

But there were some laughs, too. I think it was about this time I was sitting in the University Club of Montreal, minding my own business, when suddenly the genteel group of members drinking at the table next to mine became animated. This was unusual in that staid mausoleum. The cause was an argument over a magazine article which I had published under the name of Boris Sherashevski. The chief insurance executive of the group cried heatedly: "If Sherashevski likes Russia, he should go *back* to Russia," unaware that the putative Communist was practically at his elbow. Stephen Leacock, the founder of the Club, looked down from his portrait over my armchair, enjoying the scene.

At this time, too, I used to drive out to Gardenvale, near Montreal, to talk to James Harpell, said to be a dismissed Sun Life salesman, who was running a small publishing house and putting out the *Journal of Commerce*. Harpell, by this time getting somewhat old and crotchety, had been fierce enough as a youth. As early as 1906 (the same year the Armstrong Committee published its ten-volume report demolishing the moral pretensions of the life-insurance industry in the United States), he had published an outspoken criticism of the management of Canadian life companies, with particular attention to Sun Life. It is delightful to contrast the 1905–14 volumes of Sun Life's sweetness-and-light magazine, the *Primrose*, with the harsh actualities of the business as seen by Harpell.

Four years later he was vindicated, at least in part, when the Royal Commission on Insurance made its report. In four thick volumes the commission lawyers interrogated the chief officers of the leading insurance companies. Sun Life, as the largest company in Canada, and the company with nearly 50 percent of its investments in equities instead of the usual 2 percent to 6 percent, bore the brunt of the questioning. Robertson Macaulay, the president, and his son T. B. Macaulay, heir apparent to the presidency, each spent several days on the stand.

Summed up twenty-two years later in *Hansard,* the charges made in 1910 by the Royal Commission on Insurance against the Sun Life company were:

1. Improper transfer of funds.
2. Defective methods of bookkeeping.
3. Dangerous investments.
4. Total disregard of the supervision of the Department of Insurance.

The results, as quoted in *Hansard* for March 14, 1932, read:

> It is plain to your commissioners that the large interest of the Sun Life Assurance Company in these various enterprises is greatly in excess of the limits of reasonable investment.

The report concludes by stating:

> The accumulation of so large a contingent fund, earned by the speculative use of the moneys of the company, included for the most part policyholders' money—especially without giving the present policyholders the benefit thereof—is, in the opinion of your commissioners improper.

In 1932, Sun Life, having continued to ignore the suggestions and threats of the Department of Insurance about its investment policy, found itself properly up a tree. Between 1929 and 1932 its surplus had dropped from $60 million to under $6 million; new insurance written dropped from $705 to $216 million, both bond and equity investment portfolios were at unheard-of lows, and people had stopped paying interest to the company on their mortgage loans. To make matters worse, the company was bleeding to death from a massive increase in policy loans: $27 to $58 million between 1929 and 1933!

In time's nick, the last possible day for saving the company, December 31, the Bennett government suddenly passed an Order in

Council saying that Canadian life companies could use share prices as of June 1 rather than the usual December 31, 1931, for valuation of their assets. Opposition members of Parliament such as Mitch Hepburn immediately pointed out the obvious (also quoted in *Hansard*, March 14, 1932):

> The action of the Prime Minister can be taken only in one way; the company was insolvent; he resorted to the powers given him by parliament to save the situation, and so the statement was presented in its present form.

He went on to outline the financial situation of the company, and declared:

> In other words, the Sun Life Assurance Company, according to its own statement, not Mr. Harpell's, would show a depreciation of approximately $200,000,000 of its assets, which total $624,000,000. So that the company's assets are impaired to the extent of between 35 and 40 per cent.

Hepburn went on to support another charge that Harpell had been hammering away at for years—namely that the Macaulays, father and son, as chief shareholders of the company, had been less than scrupulous in balancing the interests of shareholders versus policyholders.

Macaulay had been accused of double-dealing before. He had tried to get government permission to increase the capitalization of Sun Life but had been refused. Hepburn says:

> As a member of the banking and commerce committee I remember hearing Mr. Macaulay say that the reason for the application for increased capital was that Americans were secretly getting control of the capital stock of the company. We made an investigation, and Mr. Finlayson's evidence was to the effect that the president of the Sun Life Assurance Company, Mr. Macaulay, transferred to New York 780 shares of his own stock in order deliberately to misrepresent the situation before the banking and commerce committee. I ask hon. members what they think of the head of a great financial institution who would deliberately transfer his own shares in trust to the United States and then come back and misrepresent the whole transaction to a committee of this house in order to obtain an increase of capital. As I

said before, this increase of capital would have had a marketable value of about $50,000,000, and the old shareholders would have benefited to the extent of about $48,000,000.

There was no effective rebuttal of these serious charges, damaging as they were to the party in power, and to the Sun Life management. The Parliament, in these deliberations of March 14, 1932, seemed to be vindicating all that Harpell had been saying in the *Journal of Commerce* for some years. But just nine months later he was convicted of criminal libel on charges laid by T. B. Macaulay himself, and had to put up a bond to keep the peace.

Harpell himself went to his grave convinced that what he had said in his books (see Bibliography) was the simple truth, and that some day Canadians would come to see that he had served their interests well. It hasn't happened yet.

In 1962 one of my books on finance got on the best-seller list. This motivated my then publisher to ask if I had anything else, and the answer was yes, my manuscript about the life-insurance industry, copies of which had been circulating in samizdat form for nearly twenty years. After lots of production ennuis it was finally issued in 1964 as *Life Insurance: Benefit or Fraud?* At Christmas the previous year, I ended a long letter answering editors' queries:

> Dear friends, do not let's panic. This is a difficult book and a difficult subject. No one knows the difficulties better than I. But I think all the cases given can be authenticated to your satisfaction, and if they can't we can remove them and substitute simpler cases. I am sure the world is now ready for this book, and it will reflect credit on both author and publisher.

This last proved to be true, as the book collected praise and blame for years, and had to be reprinted twice, because it kept disappearing mysteriously from public libraries.

More important, the book had at least one serious reader. René Lévesque, at that time a member of the Lesage cabinet, called me one day to say he had read the book and wanted to have a talk with me. I met him in the Spartan surroundings of the Hydro-Québec cafeteria, where he chain-smoked while studying a well-marked-up copy of my book. We spent a couple of hours going over what he thought might be inconsistencies, and discussing my current views about government insurance schemes. I left the meeting thinking that something might come of it. I was mistaken.

Lévesque was unique in actually reading the book through. The normal thing is to do nothing. In all my books I try to devote Chapter 12 to some discussion of what should be done to alleviate the effects of disasters previously revealed. Of all the books I have sent to prime ministers in Ottawa and premiers in Toronto, Quebec City, Winnipeg, and Victoria, only two got noticed. Lévesque had questions. Diefenbaker looked up his name in the index of *Ideas in Exile*, and wrote me a letter threatening to sue for libel!

There was some minor fallout from the life-insurance book. The Toronto *Telegram* staged a full-page debate between me and Andrew Elder, president of the Life Underwriters' Association, but continued to publish the misleading full-page ads of the life-insurance companies. The best fun of the late sixties and early seventies was my libel suit against J. R. Gorman, manager of Confederation Life's main office in Montreal. About 1963, when gathering material for the book and trying to pry the companies loose from their rates, I sent out a questionnaire to many companies. One of the standard replies I used to get from insurance-company people was the abusive telephone call. When I am dealing with insurance companies and their hired men I always record the conversations, so I had in my files a clear transcript, in Gorman's own words. After our talk he made a deal with the editor of a paper called *En Ville*. Confederation Life would buy advertising space for actual money, on condition that the editorial page print a libelous squib written by Gorman about me. The starving editor leapt like a startled gazelle at this good news, and in no time the money changed hands and the deed was done.

The article, which purported to be editorial matter but appeared on the same page as advertisements from Confederation Life and Sun Life, was a poorly written, scurrilous libel on one H. H. Green. Green lived in the Town of Mount Royal, was a professor, and had committed the crime of trying to obtain price disclosure from Confederation Life. The titles of his published books were suspiciously close to my own. I particularly objected to Gorman's comparing me to Hitler and Goebbels.

I asked my lawyer to sue for libel, partly because I thought I might get some redress from the law, but mostly because I thought the life-insurance industry in general, and Confederation Life in particular, should be put on notice that I, unlike most people, would not take this kind of activity lying down. Gorman, in his sworn statement in response to my suit, denied that he had written the article, or that he had ever seen it before it was published in the newspaper.

Nine years later the case finally came up in Superior Court before the Honourable Mr. Justice F. R. Hannon. In the interval *En Ville* had bowed to the discrepancy between its advertising revenues and its costs, and had sunk below the surface of the corporate ocean. The editor, Myer Gutwillig, was now a real-estate salesman. Gorman was no longer head of the Confederation Life agency, but had become a trust officer with Montreal Trust.

Plaintiff and defendants told their stories in turn. Gorman, under oath, denied that he had written the piece or had prior knowledge of it; yet Gutwillig testified that Gorman had indeed handed him the article and the money for the Confederation Life advertisement.*

In his judgment, Justice Hannon mentioned the perjury only incidentally, saying Gorman had under oath "denied any connection at all with the article". He found that there was undoubtedly libel, but, noting my Monaco tan, said I had been hurt more in my feelings than in my pocketbook, and accordingly awarded me damages of $500 and costs. After paying my lawyers' bills, I had a net loss of only $1,000 and plane fare.

In the seventies my pretty blonde daughter-in-law, Ann, was delighted to get a job, because her husband was at McGill, and they needed the money. She was the receptionist at the main office of Crown Life in Montreal. Three days after she had settled in at the job one of the bosses came up and said to her: "Do you happen to be any relation to the J. J. Brown who writes books on life insurance?" She said he was her father-in-law. She was fired on the spot.

Finally (or maybe not finally) in 1982 I published a new book on finance with Jerry Ackerman, which (as all books on personal finance must) touched on the life-insurance game. The reviews across Canada were uniformly enthusiastic, except in Montreal, where a *Gazette* staffer, one Enchin, produced a misleading and childishly personal squib. I was willing to shrug off the libels, judging them by their source, but one devastating misstatement in the review had to

---

*For a transcript of the dramatic moment leading to the proof of Gorman's perjury, see Appendix 7.

be fought. Enchin had not liked my idea of buying term insurance and investing the resulting premium savings in a separate account. In ridiculing it, he said the table of Occidental Life term premium rates in the book was false: "you can't buy insurance at these rates anyway." It seems impossible that an experienced newspaperman could be that ignorant, but I have been assured he could.

My registered letter to the editor didn't even receive the elementary courtesy of an acknowledgement. So when I returned to Montreal in June I went down to the *Gazette* office to try to see the Editor. He was too busy, but I did succeed in pressing into the hands of his secretary a printed rate list from Occidental, proof that you *can* buy life insurance at these rates. I also complained to the *Gazette* ombudsman, Clair Balfour, but so far he has been too busy investigating complaints less close to home.

What I have tried to show in this chapter is that my own experience, limited in time to a forty-year period, confirms the verdict of history that the life-insurance industry as a whole, and many of its individual practitioners, have moral standards that leave much to be desired. Not only do they publish false and misleading material about insurance ("permanent", "guaranteed", "level premium") outside the courts, but some even perjure themselves within; they use underhanded means to suppress those who try to speak the truth about insurance; they use their influence in high places to get rid of their enemies; they use their policyholders' money to influence legislatures; and they seduce newspapers with lucrative advertising contracts.

# Chapter 11 Some Adverse Social Effects of the Life-Insurance Industry

*But with nobody to account to,
and behind all its sententiousness
no true sense of public service, the
'non-profit' life insurance industry has betrayed our confidence.
Insurance leadership has passed
the buck right back to the public.*
      GOLLIN,
      *Pay Now, Die Later*, p. 179

There are two ways of proving that a business is noxious: you can look at the product, and what it does to consumers, or you can study the things that have happened to society because of the actions of the industry. Both approaches should be taken with life insurance, and both yield hair-raising results.

From the consumer's point of view, the most important points are the price scandal, including the lack of full disclosure, the overselling by misrepresentation, and the agency system.

Life insurance is about the only business left whose profits are secret. The life-insurance industry has always played its cards close to its chest. And not without reason. The law says the companies must report on operations to the Department of Insurance of each province, and they do. But the Superintendents of Insurance don't ask the right questions, and, moreover, are very coy about giving out information.

It may be that now, with the Freedom of Information Act, more facts will be available, but you can be sure that nothing like full disclosure will take place without a lot of reformers pushing. Before you can think straight about life insurance you have to understand that it is quite different from any other service or production industry. A key difference is: the life companies do their best to hide basic facts about the industry from consumers.

Can you think of any other industry that makes a secret of how much it charges for its services? Consumers' Union of United States Inc. has been devoting its resources and skills to exposing this problem for forty years, and now in the 1980 edition of its *Report on Life Insurance* has finally got it licked. Before going on to give detailed price comparisons naming company names with the best placed first, Consumers' Union has this to say:

> Suppose that car buyers were never told the price of a car, just the monthly payment. And suppose that the monthly payment turned out to be roughly the same for most cars. It would hardly be a surprise to find many a Rolls-Royce, Mercedes-Benz, and Jaguar on the road, with rarely a Chevrolet in sight. Suppose further that what the buyers didn't know, and weren't told, was that the Rolls-Royce payments, say, were on twenty-year loans rather than three-year loans, that the Mercedes payments covered interest only, and that the Jaguar payments were for leases, not for purchases.
>
> Absurd? Of course. And absurd is the only word to describe the way many consumers must decide which life insurance policy to buy—without full understanding of a policy's projected cost. Agents and companies rarely educate consumers on how to take advantage of what cost information there is available. And much of the insurance industry is reluctant to disclose additional cost data. Because cost information is limited, many buyers focus solely on the premium. That's how, in the life insurance industry, companies can sell as many policies at Rolls-Royce prices as at Chevrolet prices.
>
> One wonders how consumers would react if General Motors said that it would cost too much to figure out the price of a Chevrolet, and that all the consumer really needs to know is the monthly payment. If it weren't so serious, it might almost be funny. The life insurance industry offers a purely financial product. Yet, faced with demands to disclose in detail the price of its product, large segments of the industry are still able to duck disclosure and evade the obligation to provide comprehensive and comprehensible cost information.

This is well illustrated by the results of my industry surveys in 1945, 1963, and 1983, in which I tried to get a straight answer to a simple question: How much do sixty representative companies charge for common types of insurance? In the 1963 survey I sent out a letter and a simple form. I did all the work arranging the material; all the company had to do was get a clerk to fill in the form from the rate book.

If I sent a letter to General Motors, Ford, Chrysler, and American Motors, saying I was interested in prices and factory options, you can be sure I would get an answer from each company, and probably some calls from salesmen besides. In the 1963 life-insurance survey I did get some telephone calls from insurance salesmen; but instead of telling me about the service they had to sell, they called me a Communist, said they had heard of my type of person before (whatever that means), and refused point-blank to give the information.

Only nineteen out of sixty companies had the common business courtesy to reply to my letter. Of the nineteen replies, six (Equitable, Canada, Fidelity, Dominion, CUNA Mutual, and Manufacturers) completed the form in full and without argument; one (Prudential of America) sent sample rates; one (Crown) sent a letter of query about the form.

But the vice-president of New York Life wrote me saying the information I wanted was "not available"! Prudential of England wanted to know if I was willing to contribute to the cost of filling out the form! Three companies asked why I wanted information on how much policies were going to cost me, implying that it was none of my business; three others had local salesmen telephone me, asking the same question. When I told the salesmen I was writing a book on life insurance, they became quite abusive, because this is a taboo subject. Three other companies (Metropolitan, Imperial, London) said: "Ask your friendly local agent."

There is good reason for life companies remaining tongue-tied and coy about prices. Where else can you be persuaded to buy $1,000 worth of protection for either fifty cents or a hundred dollars?

This question of full disclosure is critical. I see myself in the tradition of the apostolic succession of critics of the life-insurance business. This is a long and honorable line, beginning with my fellow Canadian Morris Robinson in the 1840s, then Elizur Wright, Pateman, Abree, Johnson, Harpell, Brooks, Armstrong, Brandeis, Epstein, Berman, Campbell, the Gilberts, Green, Hughes, Kidder, Siegel, Torrens, White, Guillet, Sherashevski, Langstaffe, Hendershot, McIntosh, Reynolds, Stowers, Gollin, Consumers' Union, Rudd, Belth, Shulman, and McLeod. The latter, another Canadian, brings us full circle in 1981. These are the men who made it possible for you to buy term insurance, who introduced the non-forfeiture laws, the idea of mutualization (in the 1850s a great idea, no matter how corrupted it is today), and so on. What these men did can be found in their books listed in the Bibliography, and in the index.

Insurance salesmen are not the only ones who oversell by misrepresentation, but, having sold you too much, they are the only industry that absconds with *all* your money when you come a cropper with their over-ambitious plan. The agency system, based on the unexamined cliché "Life insurance has to be *sold*", has been with us for four generations. Everyone agrees that it makes for high-cost low-coverage insurance, but the industry insists that it is the only way insurance can be sold. If they really believed this, they would have the magnanimity to permit experiments such as savings-bank life insurance, continuing protection for former servicemen, mail-order, or across-the-counter selling. But, as usual, they are mistaken. At the same time as they are saying that only the agency system will work, they are fighting hard behind the scenes to have their captive legislatures prevent competition.

Gollin, the life-insurance executive quoted at the head of this chapter, believes that the worst thing about the agency system is the waste of human resources. I am also concerned about the waste of policyholders' money. Together they produce an environment of extreme uncertainty. This is precisely the wrong atmosphere for serious discussion of personal finance. Gollin says, in *Pay Now, Die Later*:

> In almost every one of the thousands of life insurance agencies, salesmen are driven to commit fraud and near-fraud in order to keep on validating their so-called salaries. The agent who is under such pressure finds it temptingly simple to falsify his figures.

Compare the insurance-company ads (you paid for them) with the reality. New York Life shows you a handsome male model, and says: "The agent in your community is a good man to know." But *what* agent? The turnover figures for salesmen in this industry are horrendous. Gollin, from within the industry, believes that nearly 90 percent of sales recruits leave the field within ninety days. Companies resist any talk about the cost of recruiting the 200,000 new salesmen who are brought into the industry each year. And well they might. If it is true that the average man buys insurance seven times in his life, each time from a different salesman, there is something basically wrong with the system.

The other usual approach to proving a business noxious is to look at how its assets and profits have grown over the years. If a business provides a service and takes a fair profit for so doing, it is unlikely to come up with growth figures like the following:

—The annual take from the stream of post-tax disposable income reached $3.5 billion in Canada in 1981.
—Total assets in the United States jumped from $2 billion in 1900 to $350 billion in 1978.
—Annual sales went from $1.5 billion to $400 billion in the same period.

The basic problem of the life-insurance industry today is that it has accumulated so much money by price-gouging for more than a century that it doesn't know where to turn. Look around your home town. The tallest, most modern glass-and-marble business palaces are usually the home offices of insurance companies. The income-tax department takes the view that it is fair to make a personal assessment of individuals based, not on the income declared, but on the apparent income as expressed in the number of Rolls-Royces you display and the size of your homes. If this criterion were applied to the life companies, everyone would have to agree that excessive levels of profitability have been in force for some time.

Even if the right kind of insurance were being sold at a reasonable price, to the right people at the right time, through an efficient and modern sales system, I would still advocate complete elimination of the industry. The reason for this is its many adverse effects on society, some of which are on a scale that is hard even for governments to control. Life insurance is, after banking, the largest single industry in both the United States and Canada, and it has proven one of the hardest industries to regulate. The larger it gets, the more difficult it will be to bring it under the supervision of a federal department like the Securities Exchange Commission.

### The Importance of History When Discussing Life Insurance

The whole point of the historical approach is to show that the life-insurance industry, unlike other industries, has not improved greatly over time.

In England in the eighteenth century—then as now a bookie's paradise—everybody was a bettor. Just as insurance companies were being started, some bright souls had the idea of insuring someone without his knowledge and then hiring a thug to kill him. They then, as beneficiaries, pocketed the death benefit. This was a great business financially, but the moral overtones left something to be desired. It took government and the industry 100 years to put an end to this scandal. It was only in the 1850s that you had to prove insurable interest before you could take out a policy on someone's life.

After this savory beginning, anything could happen. And it did. In England, as late as the early nineteenth century, policy owners who had fallen on hard times and could not pay their premiums were auctioned off in public. The highest bidder then became the owner of the policy, the former beneficiaries were cut off, and the new owner had a financial interest in seeing that the policyholder's remaining days were numbered. Of course, I am not suggesting that murder is still going on. The industry has found more socially acceptable ways of turning an honest penny. But every generation since 1790 has seen government investigations of the life-insurance industry, all resulting in severe criticisms. See Appendixes 1 and 2.

The abuses pointed out by Charles Evans Hughes in the early years of this century are still going on, perhaps not as brazenly as they were in 1904, but still there in principle, and much more important now because the absolute dollar amounts are so much larger. The Temporary National Economic Committee investigations of 1936 and the FTC investigation of 1973 both pointed out abuses in the fields of secrecy, conflict of interest, price-gouging, calculation of reserves, and misleading advertising, but nothing was done. The companies simply ignored the criticisms, and carried on business as usual.

In the past, some industries have reformed themselves from within; others have been reformed from within by union action; still others (small loans) have been reformed by legislative action. Life insurance is the only remaining major industry that does not have to disclose prices charged and interest yielded on deposits, or executive salaries and bonuses, or its mark-up.

There are basic problems in the life-insurance industry that, in my view, make it inevitable that every few years it must break out in a horrendous scandal. For example, there is a basic conflict of interest between the management and the policyholders, particularly in the so-called "mutual" companies. The managers want the company to *grow*, to justify higher salaries for themselves; the policyholders' interests would be best served by having the company *shrink* (that is, sell off its assets and pay the policyholders a huge dividend). This basic conflict has never been acknowledged.

Carruthers, in his 1973-75 report on his insurance study for the Ontario government, has a good summary of the industry problems, couched in delicate legal language. He recommends the following major changes:

—full disclosure of prices
—a body of independent consultants to help consumers
—new approaches to marketing (getting away from the wasteful and expensive agency system)
—disclosure of expected value of monetary benefits
—disclosure of the company's performance record on "dividends"

His emphasis on "disclosure" indicates to me that his experience, like mine, was that the companies don't tell. And his proposal for a body of independent consultants suggests that he agrees with me that consumers need help.

This basic pattern of regular scandals can be seen in Appendixes 1 and 2, but the most recent breakout came in 1973 with the scandal of the Equity Funding Life Insurance Company.

Back in 1960 a new company had been founded to sell life insurance in a new way. The customer was to be persuaded to buy a mutual fund, and then to use his equity in the mutual fund to secure a loan which would pay premiums on a conventional life-insurance policy. This way he would get his life-insurance protection "free", and, in addition, if there were a rising market for stocks, he would enjoy a capital gain on the mutual fund. The holding company, Equity Funding Corporation of America, somehow got listed on the New York Stock Exchange, and by 1973 its wholly owned life-insurance and mutual-fund companies claimed to have assets of $750 million. By then, the stock, largely owned by the founders and the original underwriters, was selling for $80 a share.

No matter how you pay for it, equity-funded or cash, permanent life insurance is still an antique and obsolete system of combining insurance and savings in one contract. So it was only a matter of time before Equity Funding Corporation had to crash. In 1971 a company employee had gone to the SEC's Los Angeles office with proof that massive fraud—forgery of life-insurance policies for resale, forgery of death certificates, forgery of bonds—had taken place. He asked for immunity from prosecution in exchange for his proofs, and the SEC refused. Then nothing happened for over fourteen months, and the stock continued to rise. In January 1973 Ronald Secrist, who had been fired by the company, went to Raymond L. Dirks, a leading security analyst specializing in life-insurance stocks. Dirks, the author, with Leonard Gross, of the best-selling *The Great Wall Street Scandal*, knew proof when he saw it: Secrist alleged that Equity Funding had created thousands of fictitious life-insurance policies, then had sold these policies to other companies; that the company had made up fake death certificates; that it had created fake assets and counterfeit bonds; that the officers of the company not only were involved in the plot but were its architects; that middle management carried out the fraud knowingly; that a substantial number of people inside and outside the company knew about the fraud; and that the fraud had evolved because of a need to boost the price of Equity Funding stock so that the company could acquire other companies through a trade of shares. The acquisition of profitable companies could cover up the lack of profitability inherent in the Equity Funding operation.

As soon as Dirks was able to get this news to his corporate clients, the stock collapsed and was withdrawn from trading, and the corporation disappeared behind the protection of Section X of the Bankruptcy Act—the second-largest corporate bankruptcy in history.

Twenty-two former officers and auditors of the corporation have been convicted on various charges of fraud, forgery, theft, and conspiracy. Similar trials took place in Illinois, the seat of the largest of the Equity Funding life-insurance companies, and more jail sentences were meted out to the erring top executives.

The criminal trials, appeals, and civil suits are still not completed, but to date six of those charged have begun serving their jail sentences.

It can be argued that the Equity Funding Life Insurance Company scandal was one of those unfortunate things that can happen in any industry, and it has no significance that is intrinsic to the life-insurance industry as a whole. I believe, on the contrary, that the conditions I have outlined in the life-insurance industry provide a fertile ground for corruption. This is because the tension and the conflict of interest provide a constant temptation, and every once in a while the management goes too far. I am happy to be able to say that an expert of Dirks's caliber agrees with me.

The major counts in my personal indictment of the life-insurance industry come under the following ten headings:

## 1. Inhibition of capital formation

In a free society, new businesses are created when men, money, and machines are put together at the right time. Ideas are a dime a dozen, machines and men can be found, but raising capital for a new business has always been very difficult. Before the life insurance industry achieved such a grip on society, it was easier to raise money for a new venture. Your neighbor or your brother-in-law had control of his own savings, and was in a position to help you get started. New businesses created employment, and everyone benefited.

Capital formation is the key to making capitalism work. Today the classic means of capital formation are inhibited by huge corporations, most notably the life-insurance companies. They take the small savings of millions of individuals and mismanage them in such a conservative way that they can perform next to no function in getting new industries started. So governments try to fill the gap, and, since they are run by civil servants, not businessmen, they make a mess of it, losing further millions of the taxpayers' money.

This matter of capital formation should be the main item on the conscience of life-insurance executives. But it is not. They take full-page ads (with your money) telling you that "it's good citizenship to own life insurance" and delivering themselves of clichés about industrial democracy, but the truth is they themselves are a major obstacle to making democratic capitalism work. I claim that their inhibition of capital formation leads to high levels of unemployment, with all its attendant social problems.

## 2. A drag on the business community

The checkered history of the insurance industry, featuring scandal, corruption, fraud, thievery, and even murder, has done its bit to give the rest of the business community a bad name. It took the courts nearly a hundred years to put an end to murder in the insurance business, but the exaggeration and double-dealing are going right on. The fact that you can become a top executive in life insurance, and receive a top salary and top benefits, without much education, or native skills, or even working very hard, is demoralizing to the rest of the community.

Some insurance people make no bones about it. With startling frankness, Irvin Pitch (what a perfect name for an insurance salesman) writes, in *The Pitch Formula for Success* (p.13):

> I soon realized that a career in life insurance sales would give me the opportunity for financial growth, personal leadership, and community recognition *without having to go through the rigors of formal education*.

It shouldn't be a surprise, then, that some life companies boast the worst management in the whole business community. This is important, so don't take my word for it. James Gollin, author of *Pay Now, Die Later*, is a former insurance-company executive, and knows the business well. He calls it "our biggest and most wasteful industry", and cites chapter and verse in the areas of underwriting, administration, advertising, and marketing. He sums up: "of all our private enterprises, life insurance is perhaps the best entrenched, most privileged and most powerful. Its misfunctionings, malodorous marketing practices, and unresponsiveness to the public welfare are studies in our system at its worst."

Shulman, in *The Billion Dollar Bookies*, has systematic milking of policyholders as his main topic. The pious mismanagement and scandalous inefficiency that go on behind the cover of "mutualized" companies is well known to the rest of the business community, and is covered by my friend Scott Reynolds, as well as by *Fortune* magazine, Brandeis, Shulman, Dorfman, and Rudd.

Speaking of the panic of April 1980, when there was a run on the

life-insurance-company reserves that reached an estimated $40 bil-
lion, *Fortune* says:

> The industry has also been exposed as wildly vulnerable to steep
> increases in interest rates. This winter and spring, as rates rose, the
> winds of change resembled a tornado, spinning many companies into a
> cash-flow bind and shattering their executives' confidence. The recent
> precipitous decline in interest rates has eased the industry's problems,
> leaving it limp with relief. But insurers also deeply fear a new surge of
> inflation. To protect themselves, says Robert T. Jackson, chairman of
> Phoenix Mutual, they have little more than "feeble, ineffective strate-
> gies". (July 14, 1980, p.86)

The disruption of capital and equity markets is best documented in
the reports of the Armstrong Committee (1908), TNEC (1940), FTC
(1973), and other government investigations, but is also found in
books on corporation finance, such as Dewing, and Graham and
Dodd.

The examples outlined above, covering uneducated executives,
pious frauds, managerial inefficiency, and disruption of equity markets, lie behind the feeling I have heard businessmen express—namely
that the insurance industry is a drag on the business community as a
whole.

### 3. Cosy deals with public officials

The co-opting of regulators by the regulated is by no means confined
to the life-insurance industry, but in both Canada and the United
States insurance people have developed it to a fine art. It is so
common that it even has a special name. It is called the "revolving
door". When a Department of Insurance man is looking for a job, he
often finds it within the industry; when a life-company man wants
the peace and quiet of the civil servant, he gets a job with the
Department of Insurance. This cosy situation, where the regulator
and the regulated are all old friends, is nothing but bad news for the
consumer. Not only are his interests not likely to be protected as a
result of the collusion, but the whole costly deal is at his expense!
Needless to say, not all government officials are corrupt. My own
forty-year experience in trying to squeeze information out of Superintendents of Insurance has not been a happy one, but William
McLeod, the Canadian author of *Life Insurance and You,* tells me he

is enjoying increasing cooperation from both federal and provincial departments. If this marks a permanent change, it is good news for consumers. But again, don't hold your breath.

For seventy-five years there has been a struggle in the United States to prevent regulation of life insurance by the federal government. Centralized control was strongly recommended by the Armstrong Commission in 1906, as it has been by every investigating committee since. But the insurance companies could see that regulation by fifty disorganized and competing state departments would be far better for them, and they immediately set up effective lobbies to fight the federal plan. As a result, life insurance is the only major financial industry today that is *not* subject to federal regulation.

In Canada a federal Department of Insurance exists, but it is careful not to ask the life companies any of the questions that *matter*. These include:

1. How much do you charge for protection and what is your mark-up?
2. What is your lapse rate broken down by type?
3. What is your breakdown of sales and promotion expenses?
4. What salaries and bonuses do you pay your executives?

Brazen interference with the legislative process, using *your* money to achieve the company's goals, is one of the most despicable of life-company activities. They learned early on how to influence legislators, auditors, and public servants, and every investigation from 1905 to 1975 makes a major point of this. Between 1910 and 1920, the life-insurance lobby in Albany took the form of a magnificent whorehouse near the state legislature, where the lawgivers came to be influenced. Having infiltrated the state-insurance departments that were supposed to police the industry, and achieved control of the legislature, the life companies could do as they wished. The whole industry is a living rebuttal to the old saw: "Cheaters never prosper."

Government attempts to regulate the excesses of the life-insurance industry are not an unbroken record of failure. Elizur Wright's first major book in the mid-nineteenth century forced the companies to adopt his system for making sure that the companies were at least actuarially solvent; looting of the treasury by large shareholders was stopped; and just recently (*Barrons*, December 12, 1983), the Idaho and Minnesota insurance departments got together to kill a policy which had been sold to superannuated victims as a tax-avoidance scheme, but was really just an expensive cash-value policy. The retired farmers were shocked when their tax shelter suddenly turned into a cash drain, and some of them went to the cops. Academy Life Insurance Company of Valley Forge, Pennsylvania, has admitted the "deceptive use of literature" and other illegal selling tactics, and some of the old folk are going to get their money back.

But no state, provincial, or federal agency has ever been able to do much about the major scams of the industry. Carruthers names them and has some suggestions, but in the meantime life goes on very much as before. Even the relatively simple problem of controlling the excesses of individual salesmen has not been addressed. Gollin, a salesman himself and an industry executive, has this to say:

> What we try to do [said one New York State Department of Insurance complaint investigator] is make an example of one or two agents a month. We catch some guy who's clearly defrauding the public, we hold a hearing, we take his licence away, and maybe even get him indicted on a criminal charge. Then we publicize the case in the life insurance trade press.
>
> We hope that keeps the rest of the agents from really going overboard. And we do follow up on other complaints. But we can't really keep tabs on everything that's going on. There's forty of us in the Complaint Bureau and about twenty-five thousand insurance agents in New York City alone. So we pretty much have to trust the companies to police themselves.

## 4. Disruption of capital markets

As early as the 1940s, it began to be apparent, even to life-insurance executives, that the real problem of the industry was the huge pile of money it had extracted from the insured by demanding excessive reserves. Between 1920 and 1945 the amount of insurance in force had trebled, but the aggregate policy reserves had increased by a factor of six. Even in those days the absolute-dollar amounts of the reserves were staggering. F. M. Hope, vice-president and actuary of Occidental Life, wrote: "Where can the companies find investments with a decent rate of interest for such huge reserves?" Since this time the admitted assets of insurance companies have increased no fewer than fifty times!

They have now amassed so much of your money they literally

don't know what to do with it. And, not being the cream of executive types, while thrashing around under pressure to invest up to $10 million every working day in the United States, they make mistakes. Some of these mistakes are of a kind that could be made by anyone, but far too many carry with them a pervasive odor of conspiracy and fraud.

Even if the life companies are honest and scrupulous in their bond investments, the sheer size of the commitment they make to a company cannot help exposing it to dangers. At the very least, the life company puts a man on the borrowing company's board of directors. This means that the new director, if he is doing his job, is spending his time developing expertise in the airline or the pants business instead of looking after the insurance needs of his policyholders. At worst, the insurance industry becomes an octopus of finance, holding hundreds of key directorships in industries about which it knows nothing. Then, added to the normal hazards of interlocking directorships, we have the danger of fundamentally ignorant men in positions of control.

## 5. Disruption of equity markets

After the great stock-market crash, when General Motors fell from $224 to $7 and New York Central from $256 to $9, the general public became interested in regulation of the market by government bodies. The Securities Exchange Commission was set up to oversee the financial aspects of corporations, and many actual and potential swindles were prevented. Had the life companies been forced to comply with the law, it would have made public too much private information for their taste. They like the freedom of operating behind a corporate veil. So, as usual, the life companies found a way around the full-disclosure laws. Had they bought a company's stock on the open market, in the usual way, all the details of price and conditions would be known to the state-insurance department and to the SEC. Instead, to prevent this, the life companies gradually worked out a system of "private placements", under which they loaned policyholders' money to the company in exchange for a position of influence on the board. No shares were involved, hence it is no business of the SEC. Being a private placement, there is no way government or private investigators can find out about it. If this type of investment made up only a small part of the industry portfolio, it would be less serious. But in 1966 (according to the *Life Insurance Fact Book, 1966*, p. 62), of the $41 billion borrowed from the industry, $34 billion had been acquired through private placements. In 1982, the latest year such facts were available, both the absolute amount and the percentage of private placements had increased.

Gollin, writing from his vantage point as an executive within the insurance industry, was one of the first to expose the danger and hypocrisy of the private placement of funds. The system allows the industry to have it both ways: it can put on the good-corporate-citizens' front of deploring liquor, tobacco, and loan sharks, and at the same time lend huge sums to these industries through the back door. Gollin, in *Pay Now, Die Later* (pp. 149-50), gives examples of the industry selling high-priced "forced savings" plans to much public self-applause, while at the same time acting as banker to the small-loan industry, where policyholders could borrow back their own money at 20 percent interest:

> In 1964 it put $680,000,000 into these credit outfits. Needless to add, the insurance companies most active in this lending area don't advertise that they are in effect the bankers of the small-loan credit sharks. Company officials understand only too well why you might find it odd for your life insurance company (which preaches thrift and sells mostly policies that indeed *force* you to be thrifty) to finance a business that reaps its own profits from your extravagance.

As far back as 1954 I was exercised about the potential for evil held by life-insurance control over major industries. I was at that time an employee of Aluminium Limited, the holding company for Alcan Aluminum. This is a capital-intensive industry which, even in those days, spent about $35,000 for each job, and was therefore very dependent on outside capital. One of my radio programs on life insurance having raised a considerable stink with top life executives, I wrote to my boss:

> From a public relations point of view it is unfortunate that some segments of the life insurance business, particularly Mr. Leighton Foster, Secretary of the Canadian Life Officers Association, have seen fit to look upon the broadcast as an attack on the life insurance industry. I think an objective reading of the script will show that it is merely a discussion of life insurance from the point of view of the individual

who needs protection and that the pros and cons of the various methods of obtaining protection are given in a very fair manner. Mr. Dunton of the CBC has sent scripts of the broadcast to the six critics inviting them to point out specific instances of unfairness.

Life insurance people disagree violently on the merits of the standard life insurance policy which combines investment with insurance protection in one contract. The President of Occidental Life in speeches, and the company in its advertising, has come out much more strongly against this form of contract than I have ever done. I have quotations from leading executives of well-known life insurance companies saying precisely what I said in the broadcast. Therefore as to the content of the broadcast, I feel I am on very firm ground.

However, since life insurance companies form our chief market for selling our securities, we want them to like us. Industrial companies and life insurance companies have a community of interest up to a point. But when it comes to raising new equity capital, their interests diverge sharply since one is the seller and the other is the buyer. It seems to me that it is very much in our long-term interest as a company to encourage people to save through means other than life insurance policies. These other means might be mutual funds, common stocks, credit unions, or industrial bonds. If more people made use of these alternative methods of saving, companies like Aluminium Limited, when they had to float an issue of new securities, would have alternative markets in which to sell them rather than being faced with a single large buyer. Today, since one industry (life insurance) is the chief buyer of securities, our expansion policies and management activities must suit that buyer.

Henry Ford at the beginning of a new industry found it necessary to develop alternative sources of capital since the banks were too conservative to invest in the automobile industry. Since we too are in a new and rapidly expanding industry, it may be that for the longer term we would be well advised to work toward developing alternative pools of risk capital.

Now, thirty years later, there isn't much more to say. The life-insurance industry, because of its inordinate investment needs, exerts the largest single influence on all of commerce and industry. Partly because of concentration (it has been estimated that 1,000 men make the investment policy decisions for the entire industry), partly because of venality (see Appendix 2 for a list of investigations that all found wrongdoing on the part of the life-insurance industry), and partly because of sheer financial ineptness, the life companies' control over finance is a disaster for the capitalist system. It is a disaster because the enemy is within, and hidden by a thick veil of respectable public relations and persiflage.

Some readers, not familiar with the history of life insurance, will be surprised at the charge of financial ineptness, but it is not difficult to prove, or to explain. There are whole books on the investment policies of the life companies (such as Schnitman and Gollin), and the *Analysts' Journal* often takes a critical look, especially at their adventures in buying common stocks. But how could it be otherwise? For five generations life-insurance companies have stressed fixed-dollar investments exclusively, and have sneered at anyone who suggested that variable-dollar investments (common stocks) might have certain advantages. An insurance-company president allowed himself to be quoted, in 1958, as follows: "Mutual funds are speculative risks, and we only sell certainties." (Quoted in Gollin, p. 266.) As a result they have had no experience of investing in equities, and, moreover, have always developed and promoted to top positions the kind of men who would not make an equity investment in Canada at gunpoint. This is one reason why we have had to beg for foreign capital before we could develop our basic industries—the men who controlled our largest single block of investment capital were fixed-dollar men. Their competence even in this relatively simple type of investing has been questioned. After the collapse of Penn Central (a merger of two long-moribund railways, leading a declining industry to its death), it was found that by far the largest holder of Penn Central bonds was the life-insurance industry. But this makes sense too. The industry has always prided itself on its conservatism. Examples of this conservative attitude are its use of old mortality tables and its thirty-year pause to consider before it noticed the fact of inflation.

In sum, taking life-insurance men as a whole, it is difficult to think of any group less qualified by education, experience, and basic natural bent, to handle large sums of equity money.

## 6. Lack of social conscience

Most industries in a democracy tell a few fibs about their products and services, but I can think of none like life insurance, where the brazen misrepresentation of simple facts seems to be a matter of policy. A choice example, one I have treasured for years, is R.

Leighton Foster, Q.C., then the official representative of the Canadian life-insurance industry, quoted in the *Montreal Star*: "No policyholder in a Canadian legal reserve life insurance company has ever lost a dollar through non-payment of the amount guaranteed at death."\* This is easily disproved by any lawyer familiar with the basic reference books of his trade. You don't even have to be a lawyer. All university libraries and many public libraries have abridgements such as CCL (*Canadian Current Law*), *West's Ninth Decennial Digest*, and CCH *Life Cases*. These give summaries of cases under subject headings "insurance". There you can read all about such things as London Life's refusal to pay because *they* had inadvertently left the company seal off the policy! And there are hundreds more case summaries that can be read by anyone with access to a reference library.

In the United States, a much more open society than Canada in every way, there are lawyers who specialize in helping policyholders collect on their policies. They are busy men. William Shernoff, of Claremont, California, in one year (1974) won awards of $5 million (Egan case) and $2 million (Fayard case), including punitive damages. Shernoff and the California Trial Lawyers' Association are pushing a legislative bill that would allocate 25 percent of any punitive damages awarded by the courts to any agency set up by the insurance industry to watch for cases of bad faith toward policyholders. So far the industry has not come forward to support the bill.†

One of the obligations of a corporation operating in a free society, especially one that has been granted special privileges by the legislature, is to make requested information available, and to answer critics. The life-insurance industry has never deigned to do either. During its entire history it has hidden its prices and its basic statistics, and it has always had the same policy as it follows today about criticism: ignore it. This level of arrogance shows clearly what they think of their policyholders: that they are gullible fools. Even the automobile

---

\*I have recently discovered that the situation is even worse than I thought. This paragraph is italicized on page 14 of every annual issue of *Canadian Life Insurance Facts* between 1959 and 1983. This is what the industry calls "facts".

†Shernoff tells me that his book for lawyers *Insurance Bad Faith Litigation* was published in April 1984 by Matthew-Bender and Company of San Francisco. His popular book on life-insurance company swindles is making the rounds of the publishers.

industry (not one of our shining examples of corporate probity) finally got around to providing some substantive arguments to meet the criticisms of Ralph Nader and others.

This attitude of indifference to the public would be bad enough on the part of the owner of a peanut stand, but when it comes from an industry holding $350 billion of our money, an industry with its hand in everybody's pocket, it is not to be borne.

In their responsiveness to the public welfare, the life-insurance people are at least consistent. They have fought every attempt to bring the benefits of true life insurance to the people that need it. Beginning with their scurrilous personal attacks on Elizur Wright in the 1850s, moving on to their active opposition to the Armstrong, TNEC, and every other government investigation, they have arrived finally at the position that they deem themselves above the law and above social concerns.

Savings-bank life insurance was suggested by Brandeis, the famous U.S. Supreme Court justice, and others in the 1930s, and fought to a standstill by the insurance lobbies. Finally, in the 1940s, it was introduced in two states, Massachusetts and New York, but with crippling limitations on the amount of protection. This was a genuine innovation, which would have solved the problem of insurance for millions of low-income families. The industry fought it by fair means and foul as long as possible, and then agreed to accept it only in a completely emasculated form. It is still not available in Canada.

During World War II the industry put up a strong opposition to the G.I. life-insurance plan, and after the war lobbied consistently for its abolition. The idea that black people and women needed insurance was frowned upon (the argument given was that they tended to be poor credit risks). Finally, the great jewel in their crown of concern for society, they mounted an expensive campaign against the Social Security Act.

People used to say of me that I was being too severe in habitually criticizing Sun Life, the largest Canadian insurance company, and its pretentious head office in Montreal. But from the point of view of the public welfare, my criticisms are justified and accurate. They have, in their 100-year history, covered a wide gamut of anti-social activity: overselling by misrepresentation, with consequent high lapse rates; misuse of policyholders' funds to make personal profits for executives and directors; covering up their 1931 near-bankruptcy; and, finally, the spectacle of terrified little men abandoning the head office in Montreal and skulking out of the province for good. Never have I been more prescient. In a democracy, if you don't like what your government is doing, you fight it, and work for legal change. The life-insurance business has always been an autocracy, an anomaly in modern North American society, and it has no idea of how to go about acting in a democratic way.

Do I hear you saying that this is all in the past, that I am bringing up ancient history just to discredit the industry? Nonsense. The juiciest, the largest ($400 million stolen), and the most brazen of the life-insurance scandals took place just eight years ago with the Equity Funding fiasco. And the best is yet to come. Even larger scandals are on the way. As the amounts of money involved in the life-insurance game increase every year because of the huge increase in policy reserves and surplus, we can confidently expect bigger and better attempts to turn the money to private use. Remember, we are talking about sums that are larger than the national income of most European countries.

## 8. Anti-culture

Life-insurance people are book-burners. This is not a nice thing to say about any group, especially in North America, where minority opinion is tolerated, and even, in some areas, encouraged. But in my forty-year personal experience of the industry, when I kept on saying things they didn't want said, the only response the industry could mount was the suggestion that my books should be burned. I have had this suggestion in telephone tapes from disgruntled salesmen, in articles published in allegedly respectable newspapers, in courts of law, and face to face at cocktail parties. Quite apart from the basic injustice to me, a well-trained and serious scholar, this attitude poses a real danger to our open society. I am not the only author who has come in for special attention from powerful men who think it a good idea to suppress the books they do not like. Gollin begins his book with the picture of two top executives of the industry, two who up to then had helped with the book, beginning to panic and going down to Random House to lean on the publisher to see if they could have the book suppressed. His book ends by quoting a frantic, paranoic review of the book by Chester C. Nash, editor of *Insurance News*, which uses most of the space saying what a terrible person Gollin must be. Bill McLeod, author of *Life Insurance and You*, attending the annual meeting of the Superintendents of Insurance in Moncton in September 1979, was verbally attacked in the basest and most childish way by Ralph Simmons, a regional manager for London Life and president of the Life Underwriters Association of Canada. Gollin sums it up in *Pay Now, Die Later* (p. 10):

> Like too many others in their business, they behaved as if the American life insurance industry was full of important secrets that should be kept hidden. . . . I think that they and their industry do have much to hide, much to be ashamed of and embarrassed by. Certain habits and practices of the life insurance business are outrages that ought to be stopped. Although this book is by no means just a catalogue of wrongdoings, I have tried to make plain what I think is wrong, not with a few unethical insurance men or a few companies, but with the entire industry.

If we don't do something about this gargantuan and moneyed industry, it will find the brains and courage to do something to us. And that we won't like.

Samuel Johnson said there should be a book on every subject, and the cultured nations of the world, old and new, agree. Free access to the facts, and free debate on their significance, is the essence of democracy. The life-insurance industry has distinguished itself during its entire history by hiding and distorting the facts, and by bringing its vast economic and political power to bear to suppress and prevent free discussion.

# Chapter 12 Some Suggestions for Reform

*For what can be imagined more beautiful than the sight of a perfectly just city rejoicing in justice alone?*
MARK HELPRIN,
*Winter's Tale*, New York, 1983,
p. 249
(Quote inscribed on the gold and silver tray that Hardesty Maratta chose as his inheritance.)

The previous chapter will give you some idea of how bad a mess we are in because of the machinations of the life-insurance industry. The answer to the question "How big?" is even more horrendous. Berman, writing in *Consumers' Union Magazine* in 1937, nearly fifty years ago, said:

> If the big life insurance companies continue to get hold of the people's money at a rate of increase corresponding to that of the last 30 years, in another 30 or 40 years a small clique of life insurance executives and directors will control all the wealth in the U.S.

This has not happened yet, because the proportion of disposable savings entrusted to insurance companies has declined (although the absolute numbers have increased). But this does not mean the *threat* has declined. It is only in remission. Annual policy face values of life insurance in the United States in 1978 reached 20 percent of the Gross National Product. The premium income from life insurance in force in the United States in 1978 reached $80 billion, and in Canada, in 1982, it reached $3.5 billion.

## How Did We Get Into This Mess?

The quick answer is that we have rubbed universal ignorance against a realized public need, and come up with a monster. The causes of the average man's complete ignorance of life insurance are these:

—Company advertising is the only source of information.
—Moral ideas of duty and family responsibility, going back to the nineteenth century, make it difficult for us to be rational when buying life-insurance protection.
—Our TV, newspapers, and magazines do not want to offend their best customers for advertising space by telling the truth.
—The life industry systematically rejects its duties to society.
—The common man's unjustified belief that some day he will meet up with a free lunch makes him keep looking.
—The sheer magnitude and financial power of the industry silence critics.

The sacred cow didn't have its obscene growth just because we like milk. No, it has been nurtured by a unique combination of our ignorance, their unscrupulousness, and government ineptitude.

## A Modest Proposal (Again)

Forty years ago, in the persona of Boris Sherashevski, I took the view in *Canadian Forum* that term insurance should be sold by governments at the latest mortality figures, using the bodies already sitting idly in place in government buildings to do the paper-shuffling. Since then I have seen governments routinely misapply funds (taxed for one purpose, used for another), waste tax revenues, and gradually sneak in to every aspect of my life, so they know more about me than does my wife. I truly believe that big government has gone too far, and, unless we can reduce its role, we are going to have to live with permanent high unemployment, as well as other nasty things.

So it is with a slight blush that I now raise my head and say once more, "All things considered, we should ask the government to provide us with life insurance at cost." When Boris suggested this in 1945 the paperwork costs might have been high. But now, with main-frame computers already in place with lots of open time, and with software experts poised, the job becomes quite feasible at low cost. The sales cost would be zero, and the administration next to nothing, even if supervised by civil servants.

One approach might be to sell life insurance on the income-tax form. You either want it or you don't. If you do, you fill out a simple box on the form. You are allowed to buy up to three times your taxable income declared that year. The price is last year's mortality rate for your attained age. For example, at age 31 your declared taxable income was $33,300. Last year, for each 1,000 alive at the beginning of the year, 1.36 males aged 30 died. The cost, then, for $1,000 of protection is $1.36. So your premium for $100,000 of protection is $33,300×3 = $100,000×1.36 per thousand = $136. This is dirt-cheap and a great help to the hard-pressed taxpayer. Moreover, it gives non-taxpaying citizens an incentive to get on the income-tax rolls.

How much would it cost the government to provide this service? The 1981 census says there are 206,000 males alive at age 30. Say that 50 percent of them pay income tax and all of these citizens want cheap life insurance, and their average is the national family-income average of $33,300. This means the government's premium income for this age group is 103,000 times $136, or about $14,000,000. The death benefits it will have to pay out to the families of the 140 men who died would be 140 times $100,000, or $14,000,000. Since this is all done by computers in place in the tax department, the extra administration costs should be very low. All the demographic figures necessary to make it work without being crushed by an avalanche of claims already exist in the publications of government agencies.

## Some Rays of Hope

If, for some reason, your governments, state, provincial, and federal, do not want to put in the simple reform above, we are not left entirely without hope. The name of my house up north is "Almayet", short for "All may yet be well", and this expresses my faith that, in spite of evidence to the contrary, reform of spavined institutions is still possible in a democratic society. Several unique events have happened in the last few years to justify this simple faith.

Canada distinguished herself with a genuine world first when, in 1981, the Bank of Montreal took full-page ads suggesting that owners of Registered Retirement Savings Plans with other institutions should switch to the bank, because they were providing "free" life insurance. When the Canada Trust offered the same, it caused considerable hand-wringing in life-insurance circles. They don't like anyone to demonstrate how cheap life insurance *really* is.

But the most important event of recent years took place in a big country where real money is involved. In March 1983 a court decision in South Dakota allowed the big U.S. banks to sell life insurance over the counter at their thousands of branches. This is a marvellous idea that has been stymied for years by the life-insurance lobbies. Savings banks are the ideal source of life insurance for the average man. The clerks are plenty bright enough to explain the policies, yet they are on salary; hence they can afford to tell the truth. The banks are already in the business of personal financial planning, and have available insured savings programs at all levels of risk. These range from insured money-market accounts, long- and short-term savings plans, stocks with discount brokerage, and a wide range of mutual funds. This is a combination that will be hard to beat in the coming years.

Another hopeful sign is the rapid rise in group insurance, which is always term. Thirty years ago the mix of insurance sold was 85 percent individual insurance and 15 percent group. Today the proportions are almost exactly reversed.

The long-term inflationary trend is the rock on which the life-insurance industry may eventually split. The most important event since the New York State Senate investigations of 1904 is the difference of opinion between Metropolitan and Prudential, the giants of the business, over the question of variable annuities. Prudential is at last admitting that a dollar is not a dollar—that money buys less now than it did thirty years ago. Metropolitan is at least consistent; it makes the same statements today as it did fifty years ago. The split over variable annuities is, for policy-holders, the most hopeful fact about the industry.

In the United States, the life-insurance faction that has heard of inflation is getting bolder. In the October 1, 1984, issue of *Business Week*, there appeared a three-page ad, the first page saying only: "You were right! (Life insurance *was* a terrible buy.)"

Since I have been saying this for over forty years, I am naturally delighted to see it featured in a national magazine. Now that Executive Life Insurance of New York (said to be one of the top ten writers of new insurance in the United States) is confessing this for the first time in the history of the industry, there is hope for the insurance consumer in the United States. *Business Week* is not a Communist, or even a leftward-leaning, publication.

Another hopeful trend, now just beginning on the West Coast, is the personal newspaper ad. The life-insurance salesman makes his pitch and then gives his own individual name and phone number. So instead of dealing with an attractive male model (as you do in so many life-insurance ads), you are dealing with an actual person. The advantage of this is, if he swindles you by selling too much of the wrong kind of insurance at the wrong price, you can sue him for malpractice. In California, suits of this kind sometimes succeed.

Maritime Life has recently come out with a new type of policy that is giving old-line companies some bad moments. It is called a "New Money" policy, specifically an "Adjustable Single Premium Whole Life". McLeod thinks it a very useful place to put the cash-surrender value and accumulated dividends of an older policy, and he may be right for some special cases. As for me, I stick to my rule to avoid any cash-value policy. (For more information on the pros and cons of the ASPWL, see McLeod, pp. 112-14.) But the important point is that this type of policy for the first time is adding some badly needed price competition to the life-insurance industry.

### New Critics—New Worms Turning

Another development that gives me hope for the life-insurance consumer is the appearance of generalized insurance cases in the U.S. courts. Until recently all the cases had been concerned strictly with the death or disability benefit—did the company have to pay up or not? Today we are starting to get cases that go far beyond narrow points of law. As far back as 1972, William Steingart brought a class action against the four largest mutual companies, asking damages be granted to the policyholders because the company executives had fixed prices at high levels, pooled the reserves without justification, introduced misleading accounting procedures, and generally "thwarted every semblance of corporate democracy". Unfortunately, Judge Metzner threw the case out on a technicality, namely that he didn't have jurisdiction, insurance companies being regulated on the state, not the federal, level.

But the consumer hasn't lost them all. Tom Venegar, a Prudential salesman, finally caught on to the racket, and then went about converting his clients to term insurance. Other Prudential agents began what he called "a vicious personal attack" on him. Venegar made his case against both Prudential and its salesmen before the judge, and the California Superior Court awarded him $36,500 compensatory damages and $85,000 punitive damages.

Robert I. Knox sued his insurance salesman, J. Leland Anderson, for selling him a policy that cost $7,265 a year in premiums, when his total income was only $8,100. The court awarded Knox $25,000 damages, because it held that the salesman, representing himself as an "expert" and a "consultant" was required to tell Knox that the same protection could be obtained at less than 10 percent of this cost.

Of course, none of this activity has come to Canada yet, and it will be some time before it does. But our grandchildren may benefit.

## New Sources of Information

As I have mentioned, because of the Freedom of Information Act, from now on there are going to be more and better books about life insurance. For forty years I have been bugging the Departments of Insurance, federal and provincial, trying to pry some facts loose from them about how the companies spend their policyholders' money. It has been like pulling teeth. But there are signs now that the word is out that the public has the right to this information, and I am hopeful that even the companies themselves will reconsider their traditional rigid positions on price disclosures. Douglas Carruthers, the overly polite lawyer (now a judge) who was a one-man Royal Commission on life insurance for the Ontario government, went so far in his final report in 1974 as to demand not only price disclosure, but a disclosure by the companies of the mark-ups on their policies. This is still unheard of in the life-insurance industry, but I'm sure it is on its way, because new legislation has already forced the personal-loan industry to tell the truth about its interest rates.

Another good source of information that has opened up within the last couple of years is the TIAA hot-line. Teachers Insurance and Annuity Association, a respected old company that sells only to teachers at universities and schools, has set up a free consulting service that anyone can use. The number you call is 1-800-223-1200 toll-free, or 1-212-490-9000 collect.

As I have mentioned, in the Province of Quebec (and also to a lesser degree in Alberta and British Columbia) it is now possible to use a life-insurance brokerage firm to do your comparison shopping for you. This is often a good idea because they know much more about current prices than you do.

Finally, the Eaton Bay mail-order plan can be a good source of information when you are ready to buy. You do not have to face the salesman. Just fill out the form and have the monthly payment of premium (no extra charge) added to your store charge-account. You don't even have to take a medical exam.

If there is any justice, the atrociously bad management of the life companies will finally do them in. If it is true that you can't fool all of the people all of the time, then the companies must be coming to the end of the line. The mutual companies, in particular, are vulnerable to a shareholder takeover. Richard Shulman, at the back of his book *The Billion Dollar Bookies*, provides a coupon for the reader to fill in if he or she owns life insurance bought from a mutual company. In theory it is quite feasible for the policyholders to take over their mutual company simply by electing a majority of directors. But there are some practical problems. William Steingart's class action against the mutuals was dismissed in 1972, and even Consumers' Union is batting only .500 in two lawsuits it has taken against the companies. If you would like to take part in an action to replace the management of one of the Canadian mutuals with under $90 million of assets (Principal, Great Lakes, Laurier, Ina, La Nationale, Western, Reliable, Occidental, Wawanesa, and Mony), drop me a line giving your policy number. If enough policies could be represented, we could have some interesting annual meetings, and who knows, even make some money.

# Why *This* Book?

There are at least four hundred books on life insurance in English. You may well ask why, since there are already so many books published, and several of these are "buy term" books, I have gone to all this trouble to force another on an indifferent world.

The answer is that all the "buy term" books I know (and I think I have seen all but two) underestimate the difficulty of helping people change their cash-value insurance into a term-savings plan. Specifically, they underestimate the powers of the salesman and the enormous prestige of the life companies.

Typically, what happens is this. You read a book which proves to your satisfaction that the business is an unsavory racket and that you are being royally swindled by the cash-value policies you have. You decide to change to a term-savings plan. The salesman you call has seen a thousand cases like yours, and knows just how to answer or skirt your objections and beat down your arguments. In no time at all he has you tied in a knot; you find his arguments unanswerable, and decide to keep on as you are.

The unique feature of my book is that it not only exposes the legal life-insurance racket but gives you specific, step-by-step instructions on how to change over to the term-savings plan. Your opponent, the salesman, is trained to force his desires (for the commission) on you. Doesn't it make sense for you to train yourself before you can expect to force your desires on him?

I think it essential that a "buy term" book give the reader enough examples, charts, tables, and specific references to policies, naming company names, for him or her to anticipate the salesman's arguments. The amount of money the average person can save by being sensible about life insurance is $500 a year forever, and this is a lot of money. The life-insurance executives and their hired men are not going to let you take that away from them without a fight.

The 1982 report of the Canadian Superintendent of Insurance says: "Of ordinary life insurance in force at December 31, 1982, 58 percent was term, by face value." According to *Canadian Life Insurance Facts, 1983*, published by the Canadian Life Insurance Officers' Association, term made up 68 percent of all policies issued during 1982. In 1978 Consumers' Union thought that term made up about 19 percent of individual policies sold. So you take your choice.

If you include group insurance (which is convertible, but not renewable at the policyholder's option), and such gimmicks as term added to standard policies, then you can show that term makes up quite a respectable percentage of the insurance sold. But throughout this book I have insisted that any worth-while term policy is convertible and renewable without medical examination, and not mixed with any other type of insurance. By this definition, I think the amount of term sold is only about 26 percent of the total; but I can't prove it because the Superintendent of Insurance in Ottawa does not make well-defined figures available.

Clearly the "buy term" books of the past fifty years have failed in their purpose, because term still accounts for only a small part of the *individual* insurance sold. The exact percentage depends on how you define term insurance, and what basis you use for your calculations.

A good book on life insurance must give you lots of ammunition to fight with. In my view none of the "buy term" books in the following bibliography supply enough specific data to give you a fighting chance of success.

But, on the other hand, you should know about them. The fact that over four hundred books have been written about life insurance proves its importance as a subject. Many of these books were produced, like Diderot's French encyclopedia, under difficult clandestine circumstances and had to be protected by librarians to keep them from being burned. They represent an important contribution to the continuing human struggle against institutionalized evil, and as such their memory should not be lost. This is why older books that are "not available" or are hard to find are on the list that follows.

Besides, unofficial censors are at work in your public libraries, stealing "buy term" books off the shelves, or mutilating them with reprints of scabrous reviews.

The "mad Xeroxer of Mount Royal", for example, seems to be making a career out of gluing copies of a childish and misleading review of my latest book (reviewed in the Montreal *Gazette*) to the flyleaves of all my books in the Town of Mount Royal and Westmount libraries. He is a dedicated man, willing to spend long hours to keep you from learning the grim truth about life insurance.

# Selective Annotated Bibliography

*Many of these books are to be found in university libraries or in public libraries in large cities. Substantially all of them are in the New York Public Library, and your local librarian can obtain them for you through inter-library loan.*

ABREE, GEO. *Evils of Life Insurance.* Pittsburgh, 1870.
   Obsolete.

ARMSTRONG, WILLIAM W. *License to Steal.* c. 1916.
   This is in the Library of Congress, but I have never seen it. Judging by the date, it is a popularization of the findings of the New York State Joint Committee on the Life Insurance Business, 1906.

ATWOOD, A. W. *The Great Stewardship.* New York: Harper and Bros., 1945.
   Apologetics, not very cleverly done. Read it for the laugh. Atwood was an official of the Mutual Benefit Life.

BAUM, DANIEL J. *The Investment Function of Canadian Financial Institutions.* New York, 1973.
   The chapter on life insurance, "Control by Consent", is well worth reading. He has studied the debates in Parliament in 1932, when Sun Life was held up as the example that made necessary the revision of the Canada and British Insurance Act of that year. He says flatly: "[The Sun Life] was in a state of technical bankruptcy" (p. 106). On this point he disagrees with Schull.

BELTH, JOSEPH M. *Life Insurance: A Consumer's Handbook.* Bloomington: Indiana University Press, 1973.
   This is the definitive book on how to compare prices. He gives six methods, with careful criticism of each. My only criticism of his approach is that he chooses the 20-year period from age 35 to age 55 for all his price comparisons. In my view, that is far too late. Most men need their insurance when they are 20 to 30, since this is when their responsibilities are greatest.

BERMAN, E. *Life Insurance: A Critical Examination.* New York: Harper and Bros., 1936.
This is a book worth reading if you are interested in making a study of the development of life insurance. Lucid text and excellent tables. The book compares the private-enterprise companies with the Massachusetts savings-bank insurance companies, much to the discredit of the former. Berman is a college professor.

————. *Operation of Savings Bank Life Insurance in Massachusetts and New York.* U.S. Bureau of Labor Statistics, Bulletin 688, 1951. Definitive proof that even bankers can run a life-insurance business better than the life companies.

BETTGER, FRANK. *How I Raised Myself from Failure to Success in Selling.* New York: Prentice-Hall, 1949.
A "how to diddle the ignorant" book by a salesman with a cast-iron conscience. This is one of the 160 books in the New York Public Library on how to sell life insurance.

BRANDEIS, LOUIS. *Business: A Profession.* Boston: Small, Maynard, 1914. See especially the section "Life insurance, the Abuses and Remedies" (pp. 115-59).

BROOKS, C. E. *Life Insurance for Professors.* University of California Publications in Economics, Vol. 4, No. 2, 1916.
A "buy term" book directed particularly to low-income professional men.

CAMPBELL, J. G. *Concealed Weapons.* c. 1933. Published by the author, ex-agent for Canada Life Insurance Co., Saskatoon, Sask. (Parliamentary Library, Ottawa, H.G. 9010 C 35).
A turgid, emotional, anti-insurance-company book. Badly organized mixture of stiff dialogue and reprints of Superintendent of Insurance Reports for 1931 and 1932.

CANADIAN LIFE OFFICERS ASSOCIATION. *Yearbook.* Toronto.
Every year the chief insurance salesmen of Canada used to give themselves a banquet on their policyholders' money and refresh each other with mutual praises. Then they wrote it all down in a book for the delight of posterity. The policyholders, of course, paid the printing costs. This is the book. You can treat yourself to a good laugh, now that you know something about insurance, by looking at the reproductions of institutional advertising in the back.

CARRUTHERS, DOUGLAS H. *Report on the Insurance Study.* Toronto, 1975. This was a one-man Royal Commission appointed by the Ontario Government in 1973. A good summary of some of the problems, in delicate legal language that will ruffle no feathers. He calls for full disclosure of policy price, of the company's mark-up for its services, and of the company's dividends or rebate rates paid. Nice to read, but don't hold your breath.

CLOUGH, S. B. *A Century of American Life Insurance.* New York: Columbia University Press, 1946.
This is an interesting, complete, and authoritative book, giving a picture of the U.S. insurance business for the last hundred years. It is a history of the Mutual Life of New York written by an outside scholar, yet it is not without some of the usual distortions of fact practised by the life companies. But if you disregard a tendency to gloss over some of the actions of the companies, the book will be found a mine of useful information.

CONSUMERS' UNION INC. *Life Insurance*. 4th ed. New York: Holt, Rinehart and Winston, 1980.
Solid factual advice on what and where to buy, with excellent price comparisons.

DAVIES, J. P. *An Insured Investment.* International Life Underwriters Library. New York: Crofts and Co., 1930.
Davies is an insurance salesman who looks all around, and then concludes that life insurance is the best possible investment! Three years after this book was published, the U.S. government announced the Bank Holiday, which closed all banks for an unspecified length of time, and most states declared an insurance holiday too, imposing a moratorium on policy loans. This cut off the average citizen from *both* his supposed savings plans!

DIRKS, RAYMOND L., and GROSS, LEONARD. *The Great Wall Street Scandal.* New York: McGraw-Hill, 1974.
This is the definitive book on the Equity Funding Corporation of America, but it was published before the jail sentences were meted out to most of the top executives and a score of lesser fry within the company. Good to read to correct the notion that life insurance is just like any other business where sometimes there are bad apples in the barrel.

DOMINION OF CANADA. *Report of the Superintendent of Insurance*. Ottawa, Government Printing Office, annually.
Useful for anyone who makes a thorough study of insurance. Contains the official reports of all the Canadian life companies.

DOMINION OF CANADA. *Royal Commission on Insurance Report*. 4 vols. Ottawa, 1906.
Examination of Sun Life officers about their investing practices and results, pp. 2847-3054. Absorbing reading.

DUBLIN, L. I., and LOTKA, A. J. *The Money Value of a Man*. New York: Metropolitan Life Insurance Co., 1930.
It is interesting to compare what these two company actuaries have to say about term insurance (p. 147) with what the salesmen tell us.

E. J. *The Great Annual Swindle of $50 Million*. Cincinnati, 1879.
Old but fun.

EPSTEIN, A. "The Insurance Racket." *American Mercury*, September 1930.
One of the earliest exposés of the industry to get into a magazine of national circulation. One reason it was allowed to appear, of course, was that in 1930 H. L. Mencken was the editor of the *American Mercury*. The *Mercury* subsequently descended into respectability, like the rest of the magazines, and is now dead.

GANSE, P. W. *What Bankers and Trust Men Should Know About Life Insurance*. International Life Underwriters Library. New York, 1932.
Any book in this series is useless for the man who is buying life insurance for himself, because the series is designed to fortify the salesman with selling arguments. Ganse recommends endowments as investments, which sufficiently damns him. He is an insurance salesman.

GESELL, G. A. *A Study of Legal Reserve Life Insurance Companies*. Monograph No. 28 prepared under the auspices of the Securities Exchange Commission, for the Temporary National Economic Committee, Congressional Record, 76th Congress of the U.S., 3rd Session, Section XVII.
The definitive study of U.S. and Canadian company activities, since nothing has really changed since 1940.

GILBERT, M., and GILBERT, E. A. *Investing in Disaster*. New York: Reinhart, 1938.
I have read this book, but it doesn't seem to have made a lasting impression on me. I think it had something to do with the problems of life insurance facing inflation.

———. *Life Insurance: A Legalized Racket*. New York: Farrar and Reinhart, 1936.
This is perhaps the best of the old "buy term" books. The general advice to the buyer is excellent, and the book contains good analysis sheets for individual policies. The methods of policy and protection-plan analysis are good as far as they go. It is now out of print, and library copies have for the most part mysteriously disappeared. Some of the deficiencies of the Gilbert book are these:

1. It covers insurance only, and does not tell the buyer how to set up a savings plan which will gradually replace all his insurance.

2. It deals with conditions in the United States fifty years ago.

3. It does not give the reader a good simple course in understanding life insurance, beginning with the first principles. This is partly the result of the book's being a collection of separate articles which had been printed earlier in the radical magazines.

4. It gives the impression that term insurance alone will solve all your insurance problems, while in my opinion term alone can be dangerous. To be perfectly safe in dollar return, term insurance should be combined with a guaranteed frozen asset, such as an annuity or a pension plan.

5. It is not specific enough. A book on life insurance should deal with actual policies and name company names.

GOLDEN, E. T. *Young Man, Here's How to Sell Life Insurance*. New York: Harper and Bros., 1941.
This book should be read by all men before buying life insurance, to get an idea of how they are about to be manipulated. Golden, an insurance salesman, tells his readers how to milk the prospect in a nice way.

GOLLIN, JAMES. *Pay Now, Die Later. What's Wrong with Life Insurance: A Report on Our Biggest and Most Wasteful Industry*. New York: Random House, 1966, and Penguin, 1969. (All page references are to the Penguin edition.)
Gollin has been closely connected with the industry as both salesman and executive for many years. This is the best modern exposé from inside the life-insurance business. Well written and jammed with facts.

GORDIS, PHILIP. *How to Buy Insurance*. New York: Norton, 1947.
Useful, but now out of date because of falling insurance rates.

GRANT, H. ROGER. *Insurance Reform: Consumer Action in the Progressive Era*. Ames, Iowa, 1979.
Much good material on government investigations of life-insurance practices in five states (New York, Wisconsin, Mississippi, Kansas, and Texas).

GREEN, R. T. *Life Insurance Blindness*. Minneapolis, 1933, rev. 1942.
An exposé of trick life-insurance policies, including 20-pay, endowment, annuity, and many others. A "buy term" book by an independent life-insurance counsellor.

———. *A Thief in the Dark.*
I think this is a reissue, under a new title, of the "blindness" book above.

GUILLET, E. C. *Life Insurance Without Exploitation*. Published by the author, Toronto, 1946. 6th printing, 1960.

Until McLeod, this was Canada's best-known "buy term" book, but the necessity of completing the protection by the use of annuities and other savings is not stressed. The issue is further complicated by the author's getting mixed up in uplift schemes in the tradition of Sherashevski (see below). It is true that, as Guillet says, the Canadian government can provide life insurance at half the cost, but it gives no indication of doing so, and the average citizen is not much helped by this information. He has to buy insurance right now, and from the commercial companies.

HARPELL, JAMES JOHN. *Improper and Extravagant Management of a Number of Canadian Life Insurance Companies*. Gardenvale, Quebec: Business Press, 1906.

————. "The World's Greatest Crooks, T. B. Macaulay and Ivor Kreuger," *Journal of Commerce*, Vol. 56, No. 4, Feb. 1, 1930.

This series has been very effectively suppressed. There is a copy in the McGill University library, but it is more closely guarded than the Crown jewels. (T. B. Macaulay was formerly president of Sun Life.)

HARWOOD, E. G., and FRANCIS, B. H. *Insurance and Annuities from the Buyer's Point of View*. Cambridge, Mass., 1937.

This is a book which defies classification. My copy of it is annotated with nearly as many words in the margins as the authors printed in the text. They apparently began to look at insurance from the buyer's point of view, but soon found that their findings were unprintable. So the authors had to reach the conclusion at the end of the book that ordinary life is the best kind of insurance to buy. Their gyrations and contortions in reaching this conclusion are a delight to read, and I have spent many happy hours with this book. Harwood and Francis know insurance, and their book can be very useful if you read it with your wits about you.

HENDERSHOT, RALPH. *The Grim Truth About Life Insurance*. New York: Putnams, 1957.

This is by far the best U.S. "buy term" book published up to 1964. Hendershot is an expert, he knows the industry well, and besides he can write. But the book is short, and does not give the would-be twister all the ammunition he needs.

HUEBNER, S. S. *The Economics of Life Insurance*. New York: D. Appleton-Century, 1927.

A pious view of life insurance, pointing out how fine it is that the policies force the childish and incompetent working man to save.

———. *Life Insurance*. Various editions, 1917-32.
All that need be said of this book is that it was endorsed by the Education and Conservation Bureau of the National Association of Life Underwriters. ("Conservation" is the word used in life insurance for the act of persuading people *not* to turn in policies for their cash value.)

HUGHES, PINGREE C. *The Truth About Your Life Insurance*. Chicago: Association of Policyholders Inc., 1933.
Good, but rather old.

INSURANCE RESEARCH AND REVIEW SERVICE. *The Opportunity in Life Underwriting*. Indianapolis, Ind., n.d.
How to be an insurance salesman and make big money.

———. *The Technique of the Interview*. Indianapolis, Ind. Early 1960s.
Twelve books telling the salesman how to sell to the sucker. Very amusing reading if you have never been sold insurance—less amusing if you have.

JOHNSON, T. R. *Life Insurance Robbery: An Exposure*. New York, 1878.
Obsolete.

KENT, F. C. *Mathematical Principles of Finance*. New York, 1924.
Many useful tables, and some revealing information on the loading of insurance premiums (pp. 173-5).

KENTON, WALTER S., JR., C.L.U. *How Life Insurance Companies Rob You, and What You Can Do About It*. New York: Random House, 1982.
After seventeen years as a demon salesman (member of the Million Dollar Round Table), Kenton had an attack of conscience, and retired to write this book. A great modern view of life insurance from the inside.

KIDDER, JAY D. *Life Insurance: America's Greatest Confidence Game*. Seattle, 1938.

LANGSTAFFE, J. M. *Life Insurance and How to Write It*. Toronto, 1941.
Tells the insurance peddler how to make money faster.

LANGSTAFFE, M. P., and BROWN, C. W. *How to Cut the Cost of Your Life Insurance in Half*. Toronto, 1939.
This is an interesting title, but seems harder to come by than an embassy code book. None of the Toronto or Montreal libraries have it, and the bookstores have never heard of it. It is probably a "buy term" book, but I have never examined it.

LIAMA (Life Insurance Agency Management Association). Hartford, 1963.
This is a series of booklets telling salesmen how to sell. The first is called *This I Believe* and is an intensely personal, man-to-man appeal.

It is inspiring stuff, almost like a religious conversion at first hand. But typical of the sanctimonious bird-brains that can be found in this industry, it is unsigned! There is no way of finding out who is making this intensely personal appeal to you.

LIFE UNDERWRITERS ASSOCIATION OF CANADA. *Life Insurance Manual*. Toronto, 1944.
This is a little propaganda pamphlet published by the life-insurance companies for free distribution in the schools, designed to show that the Canadian life companies are on the up-and-up. The discussion is confined to vague generalities, and the authors are careful to keep away from any definite examples using figures.

LINTON, MORRIS A. *Life Insurance Speaks for Itself*. New York: Harper and Bros., 1939.
This is the best defense of the life-insurance companies it is possible to make. Linton was president of the Provident Mutual Life of Philadelphia, and a very clever man. But notice how many of the main issues of the subject he avoids entirely: the danger of inflation, savings when you buy term insurance and die young, fraudulent use of words, etc. etc. The book is a useful compendium of charges that have been made against the life companies over the past sixty years, together with more-or-less-unconvincing answers to the charges. His defense of the 6 percent rate of policy loans (p. 41) is delightful: "The 6 percent rate of interest upon policy loans has been of real assistance in confining the use of the loan provision primarily to emergency purposes. A lowering of the interest rate would of course weaken the restraining influence against the improper use of the policy loan principle."

LOVELACE, G. M. *Analyzing Life Situations for Insurance Needs: The Case Method*. Harper's Life Insurance Library. New York: Harper and Bros., 1922.
Tells the salesman how to talk men into buying more insurance than they need. How to appeal to emotions, pride, hidden fears, and so on. How to push the high-commission types. There is even a chapter on how to sell life insurance to men without dependants.

McCAHAN, D., ed. *Life Insurance, Trends and Problems*. Philadelphia: University of Pennsylvania Press, 1943.
A collection of speeches on life insurance. Notable chiefly for a delightful exposé of the net-cost argument (p. 133).

McINTOSH, FRANK S. J. *A Study of Mutual Life Insurance Dividends*. Washington, D.C.: National Analytic Service Inc., 1961.

MacLEAN, J. B. *Life Insurance*. 5th ed. New York: McGraw-Hill, 1939.
A college textbook. Maclean was actuary of the Mutual Life of New York.

McLEOD, WILLIAM E. *Shopper's Guide to Canadian Life Insurance Prices*. Toronto, 1978 and 1979.
The most serious attempt so far to make price information available to Canadians.

———. *Life Insurance and You: A Handbook for Consumer Protection*. Toronto, 1981.
This is the best recent book for Canadian readers, with solid documentation and good advice.

MAGEE, J. H. *Life Insurance*. Chicago, 1939.
A run-of-the-press book on insurance, by a salesman. Useless except for a revealing remark on term insurance which he makes on p. 419.

MASON, A. T. *Brandeis: A Free Man's Life*. New York, 1946.
Tells the absorbing story of Brandeis's investigation of life-insurance scandals, and his fight to introduce savings-bank life insurance into Massachusetts.

MATHEWSON, G. FRANK. *Information, Entry and Regulations in Markets for Life Insurance*. Toronto: Ontario Economic Council Research Studies, 1982.

MAYHEW, HENRY. "An Inquiry into the Number of Suspicious Deaths Occurring in Connection with Life Insurance Offices." *Insurance Monitor*, 4:37, July 1856, pp. 99-100.

MENGE, W. O., and GLOVER, J. W. *An Introduction to the Mathematics of Life Insurance*. New York: Macmillan, 1938.
A valuable book for anyone who is interested in a more advanced study of life insurance. The explanations are simple enough to be understood by a person with a grade-school education and a good mind, but the book takes you through the most involved actuarial problems, and is not to be read with feet on table. Many useful charts.

MOIR, H., ed. *Sources and Characteristics of the Principal Mortality Tables*. New York: Actuarial Society of America, 1932.
A fascinating but somewhat technical book for the advanced student, this is important to know about, because some companies are still using hundred-year-old mortality tables, either for valuing reserves or for setting premium rates.

MURRAY, J. ALEX., ed. *Insuring North Americans: Challenges for the 80s*. Windsor: University of Windsor, 1981.
Papers given (mostly by people in the industry) at Assumption Uni-

versity, Windsor. Considerable talk of price disclosure, comparison shopping, and other taboo subjects.

NEW YORK STATE. *Testimony Before the Joint Committee on the Life Insurance Business*. 10 vols. 1905-6.
An invaluable source book, crawling with perfect examples.

"OLD TIMER". *The Greatest Confidence Game on Earth, Commonly Called Life Insurance*. Toronto: 1906.
A "buy term" pamphlet.

PATEMAN, W. S. W. *Life Insurance: Its Schemes, Its Difficulties and Its Abuses*. London, 1852.
Completely obsolete, but useful to demonstrate how many years it takes to convince the human race it is being swindled.

PATERSON, JAMES T. *The Mystery Unveiled*. 2nd ed., St. Ferdinand, Quebec, 1889.
A Canadian pioneer in this field; now completely obsolete, but nice to know about.

PITCH, IRVIN. *The Pitch Formula for Success: Stories of a Life Insurance Agency and Its People*. Toronto: Personal Library, 1981.
Another gem from Sun Life's crown. Lots of dead giveaways about the unacknowledged conflict of interest between salesman and victim.

PORTERFIELD, JAMES T. S. *Life Insurance Stocks as Investments*. Stanford: Stanford University, Graduate School of Business, 1956.
Spectacular. Nothing has really changed in the investment side of this industry since 1956.

Q. P. *How to Buy Life Insurance*. New York, n.p., 1906.
This is probably the second "buy term" book. The modest author, "Q.P.", writes like a reformed insurance executive. Much of what he says is still true, but the book is badly out of date.

ROGERS, JAMES E. *Life Insurance for Canadians*. Vancouver: International Self Counsel Press, 1978.
Pretty disorganized, pedestrian stuff, by a life-insurance salesman who can't write.

RUDD, WILLIAM B. *Avoiding Financial Pitfalls*. Chicago: The Airline Pilots Association, 1962.

SCHNITMAN, L. SETH. *How Safe Is Life Insurance?* New York: Vanguard, 1933.
Another hard book to find. It was indexed in the old Sun Life head-office library in Montreal, but it bore no shelf mark, and was not on the shelves. From this I deduce that Schnitman's conclusion was "Not very".

SCHULL, JOSEPH. *The Century of the Sun*. Macmillan, Toronto, 1971.
A history of the Sun Life. It mentions Harpell, but not the parliamentary investigations into the company's bankruptcy in 1930.

SHERASHEVSKI, BORIS. "Security for the Citizen—A Blueprint for Government Life Insurance." *Canadian Forum*, February 1945, pp. 260-3
An article in the uplift tradition. It discusses in somewhat oversimplified terms the organization of a state life-insurance company.

————. "Government Life Insurance," *Canadian Forum*, April 1945, pp. 17-20.
A reply to critics of the state insurance plan above.

SHULMAN, RICHARD. *The Billion Dollar Bookies*. New York: Harper's Magazine Press, 1976. Published in Canada by Fitzhenry and Whiteside, 1976.
A book with a great idea, but one whose time has perhaps not yet come. He shows how owners of policies from mutual companies could get together and elect directors who would keep the companies from wasting and stealing their policyholders' money. The annual savings could then be paid out in dividends. "Vigorish" is the bookie's percentage (the difference between what he charges his clients to bet, and what he pays them if they win). The author contrasts this honest business with the mutual-life-insurance racket.

SIEGEL, MORRIS H. *Life Insurance: Fact vs. Theory*. Jamaica, N.Y.: The Foundation for Truth in Life Insurance, 1935.

SPIELMAN, PETER, and ZELMAN, AARON. *The Life Insurance Conspiracy*. New York: Simon and Schuster, 1976, 1979.
First published in 1976 under the title *Holmes and Watson Solve the Almost Perfect Crime—Life Insurance*.

SPURGEON, ERNEST F. *Life Contingencies*. London: C. and E. Layton, 1922.
This is the basic college textbook on life insurance, but you must know some calculus to get through it.

STALSON, J. O. *Marketing Life Insurance*. Harvard Studies in Business History. Vol. 6. Cambridge, 1942.
A dull Ph.D. thesis.

STONE AND COX. *Canadian Life Policy Conditions*. Toronto, published annually.
Gives the terms and conditions of life-insurance policies issued by Canadian companies, to wit: war restrictions, settlement options, total disability provisions, double indemnity, group insurance, family income benefit, and so on.

————. *Life Insurance Tables*. Toronto, published annually.
This is a very useful compendium giving, for all insurance companies in Canada, the premium rates, surrender values, dividend scales, dividend histories, financial statements, and a digest of policy conditions. The insurance companies pay to have this information published by Stone and Cox. The information is given in such form that it is difficult to compare the policies of different companies.

STOWERS, JAMES E. *Why Waste Your Money on Life Insurance?* Kansas City, Mo.: Dear Publishing Co., 1967.
Here is the truth direct from the horse's mouth. When he wrote the book Stowers was president of Survivors' Benefit Insurance Company, and knows the business well.

TORRENS, JOSEPH. *The Policyholder Loses*. New York: Policyholders' Consultants Bureau, 1939.

VAN CASPEL, VENITA. *Money Dynamics for the 1980s*. Reston, Virginia: Prentice-Hall, 1978.
Her attack on the life-insurance industry as a banking institution is now more delicately phrased, because one of her earlier books on life insurance has been banned in eight states, although it is a simple exposé of the simple truth about life insurance. Nevertheless, over a million copies have been sold and the industry can't possibly suppress them all.

WATSON, A. D. *Life Insurance and Life Insurance Tipsters*. Published by the Life Underwriters' Association of Canada, 1939, 1949, 1955.
This is a pamphlet said to be written by a former government actuary, hired by the insurance companies as an apologist. Linton (see above) is at least intelligent, and comes up with some arguments, however biased. The level of Watson's superannuated reasonings may be judged from the following: "It is rather purposeless, and misleading, to attempt...a comparison of one plan of life insurance with another, more particularly by mathematical analysis."

WHITE, DANIEL D. *Life Insurance Exposed: How to Avoid the Pitfalls of This Legalized Racket*. New York: Lenmas Publishing Co., 1938.

WOODS, E. A. *The Sociology of Life Insurance*. New York: n.p., 1928.

WRIGHT, ELIZUR. *Traps Baited with Orphans*. 1877.
The first "buy term" book, by a pioneer of the U.S. life-insurance industry.

————. *Church of the Holy Commissions*. New York, 1877.
A searing indictment of the agency system of selling.

WRIGHT, PHILIP, and WRIGHT, E. O. *Elizur Wright, the Father of Life Insurance*. Chicago, 1937.
The story of the beginning of the life-insurance business in America.

ZELIZER, VIVIANA A. ROTMAN. *Morals and Markets: The Development of Life Insurance in the U.S.* New York: Columbia University, 1979.
A good Ph.D. thesis on how present insurance marketing methods came about.

# Appendix 1 Main Government Investigations of Life Insurance

1842 First mutual company set up to correct corruption of stock companies. (U.S.)

1861 Investigation in Massachusetts resulting in non-forfeiture laws.

1870 Miller and the investigation of company financial practices. (U.S.)

1885 Kansas State Legislature investigation.

1905 Armstrong (New York State) Committee Report. 10 vols. (Hughes)

1906 Report of the Royal Commission on Insurance. Ottawa. 4 vols.

1906 New York State Joint Committee on the Life Insurance Business.

1912 Pujo Investigation. (U.S.)

1929 Royal Commission on Life Insurance, Canada.

1930 Canadian House of Commons Investigation of the Sun Life bankruptcy.

1939 TNEC Investigation, U.S. 6 vols. Report plus 2 monographs.

1941 U.S. federal investigation into the industry opposition to G.I. Life.

1973 Ontario, one-man Royal Commission (Douglas Carruthers).

1973 U.S. Senate Committee on Anti-Trust and Monopoly, Concerning Life Insurance.

1979 Select Committee of the Ontario Legislature on Life Insurance.

1980 Federal Trade Commission (FTC) report on life insurance.

# Appendix 2 Major Scandals of the Life-Insurance Industry

1715-1840 Insurable interest murders.

1830s Human auctions of policyholders, U.K.

1840s Looting of insurance companies by large shareholders. Life insurance to help carry on the slave trade. (U.S.)

1842 Equitable Life scandal.

1860s Insolvent companies. Wright investigations. (U.S.)

1870s Tontine scandals. (U.S. and England)

1875 Industrial insurance scandals: Prudential profit levels, Metropolitan lapse scandals.

1890 Hyde family scandals. Equitable Life.

1930 Concealment of the Sun Life bankruptcy.

1933 Farm mortgage foreclosures in United States and Canada.

1974 Equity Funding scandal, included regulatory bodies of three states.

1983 Governor Cuomo appoints James Corcoran, head lobbyist for Prudential, as Superintendent of Insurance for New York State.

# Appendix 3: Mathematical Tables at 8%, 10%, 12%, 15%

**RATE 8%**

| PERIODS | AMOUNT OF 1 How $1 will grow at compound interest. | AMOUNT OF 1 PER PERIOD How $1 a year will grow. | SINKING FUND Amount per year needed to grow to $1. | PRESENT VALUE OF 1 What $1 payable n years from now is worth. | PRESENT VALUE OF 1 PER PERIOD What $1 payable each year is worth today. | PARTIAL PAYMENT Annuity worth $1 today. | PERIODS |
|---|---|---|---|---|---|---|---|
| 1 | 1.080 | 1.000 | 1.000 | .925 | .925 | 1.080 | 1 |
| 2 | 1.166 | 2.080 | .480 | .857 | 1.783 | .560 | 2 |
| 3 | 1.259 | 3.246 | .308 | .793 | 2.577 | .388 | 3 |
| 4 | 1.360 | 4.506 | .221 | .735 | 3.312 | .301 | 4 |
| 5 | 1.469 | 5.866 | .170 | .680 | 3.992 | .250 | 5 |
| 6 | 1.586 | 7.335 | .136 | .630 | 4.622 | .216 | 6 |
| 7 | 1.713 | 8.922 | .112 | .583 | 5.206 | .192 | 7 |
| 8 | 1.850 | 10.636 | .094 | .540 | 5.746 | .174 | 8 |
| 9 | 1.999 | 12.487 | .080 | .500 | 6.246 | .160 | 9 |
| 10 | 2.158 | 14.486 | .069 | .463 | 6.710 | .149 | 10 |
| 11 | 2.331 | 16.645 | .060 | .428 | 7.138 | .140 | 11 |
| 12 | 2.518 | 18.977 | .052 | .397 | 7.536 | .132 | 12 |
| 13 | 2.719 | 21.495 | .046 | .367 | 7.903 | .126 | 13 |
| 14 | 2.937 | 24.214 | .041 | .340 | 8.244 | .121 | 14 |
| 15 | 3.172 | 27.152 | .036 | .315 | 8.559 | .116 | 15 |
| 16 | 3.425 | 30.324 | .032 | .291 | 8.851 | .112 | 16 |
| 17 | 3.700 | 33.750 | .029 | .270 | 9.121 | .109 | 17 |
| 18 | 3.996 | 37.450 | .026 | .250 | 9.371 | .106 | 18 |
| 19 | 4.315 | 41.446 | .024 | .231 | 9.603 | .104 | 19 |
| 20 | 4.660 | 45.761 | .021 | .214 | 9.818 | .101 | 20 |
| 21 | 5.033 | 50.422 | .019 | .198 | 10.016 | .099 | 21 |
| 22 | 5.436 | 55.456 | .018 | .183 | 10.200 | .098 | 22 |
| 23 | 5.871 | 60.893 | .016 | .170 | 10.371 | .096 | 23 |
| 24 | 6.341 | 66.764 | .014 | .157 | 10.528 | .094 | 24 |
| 25 | 6.848 | 73.105 | .013 | .146 | 10.674 | .093 | 25 |

| | | | | | | | |
|---|---|---|---|---|---|---|---|
| 26 | .092 | 10.809 | .135 | .012 | 79.954 | 7.396 | 26 |
| 27 | .091 | 10.935 | .125 | .011 | 87.350 | 7.988 | 27 |
| 28 | .090 | 11.051 | .115 | .010 | 95.338 | 8.627 | 28 |
| 29 | .089 | 11.158 | .107 | .009 | 103.965 | 9.317 | 29 |
| 30 | .088 | 11.257 | .099 | .008 | 113.283 | 10.062 | 30 |
| 31 | .088 | 11.349 | .092 | .008 | 123.345 | 10.867 | 31 |
| 32 | .087 | 11.434 | .085 | .007 | 134.213 | 11.737 | 32 |
| 33 | .086 | 11.513 | .078 | .006 | 145.950 | 12.676 | 33 |
| 34 | .086 | 11.586 | .073 | .006 | 158.626 | 13.690 | 34 |
| 35 | .085 | 11.654 | .067 | .005 | 172.316 | 14.785 | 35 |
| 36 | .085 | 11.717 | .062 | .005 | 187.102 | 15.968 | 36 |
| 37 | .084 | 11.775 | .057 | .004 | 203.070 | 17.245 | 37 |
| 38 | .084 | 11.828 | .053 | .004 | 220.315 | 18.625 | 38 |
| 39 | .084 | 11.878 | .049 | .004 | 238.941 | 20.115 | 39 |
| 40 | .083 | 11.924 | .046 | .003 | 259.056 | 21.724 | 40 |
| 41 | .083 | 11.967 | .042 | .003 | 280.781 | 23.462 | 41 |
| 42 | .083 | 12.006 | .039 | .003 | 304.243 | 25.339 | 42 |
| 43 | .083 | 12.043 | .036 | .003 | 329.583 | 27.366 | 43 |
| 44 | .082 | 12.077 | .033 | .002 | 356.949 | 29.555 | 44 |
| 45 | .082 | 12.108 | .031 | .002 | 386.505 | 31.920 | 45 |
| 46 | .082 | 12.137 | .029 | .002 | 418.426 | 34.474 | 46 |
| 47 | .082 | 12.164 | .026 | .002 | 452.900 | 37.232 | 47 |
| 48 | .082 | 12.189 | .024 | .002 | 490.132 | 40.210 | 48 |
| 49 | .081 | 12.212 | .023 | .001 | 530.342 | 43.427 | 49 |
| 50 | .081 | 12.233 | .021 | .001 | 573.770 | 46.901 | 50 |
| 51 | .081 | 12.253 | .019 | .001 | 620.671 | 50.653 | 51 |
| 52 | .081 | 12.271 | .018 | .001 | 671.325 | 54.706 | 52 |
| 53 | .081 | 12.288 | .016 | .001 | 726.031 | 59.082 | 53 |
| 54 | .081 | 12.304 | .015 | .001 | 785.114 | 63.809 | 54 |
| 55 | .081 | 12.318 | .014 | .001 | 848.923 | 68.913 | 55 |
| 56 | .081 | 12.332 | .013 | .001 | 917.837 | 74.426 | 56 |
| 57 | .081 | 12.344 | .012 | .001 | 992.264 | 80.381 | 57 |
| 58 | .080 | 12.356 | .011 | .000 | 1072.645 | 86.811 | 58 |
| 59 | .080 | 12.366 | .010 | .000 | 1159.456 | 93.756 | 59 |
| 60 | .080 | 12.376 | .009 | .000 | 1253.213 | 101.257 | 60 |

# Appendix 3: Mathematical Tables at 8%, 10%, 12%, 15% (cont.)

| PERIODS | AMOUNT OF 1 How $1 will grow at compound interest. | AMOUNT OF 1 PER PERIOD How $1 a year will grow. | SINKING FUND Amount per year needed to grow to $1. | PRESENT VALUE OF 1 What $1 payable n years from now is worth. | PRESENT VALUE OF 1 PER PERIOD What $1 payable each year is worth today. | PARTIAL PAYMENT Annuity worth $1 today. | PERIODS |
|---|---|---|---|---|---|---|---|
| **RATE 10%** | | | | | | | |
| 1 | 1.100 | 1.000 | 1.000 | .909 | .909 | 1.100 | 1 |
| 2 | 1.210 | 2.100 | .476 | .826 | 1.735 | .576 | 2 |
| 3 | 1.331 | 3.310 | .302 | .751 | 2.486 | .402 | 3 |
| 4 | 1.464 | 4.641 | .215 | .683 | 3.169 | .315 | 4 |
| 5 | 1.610 | 6.105 | .163 | .620 | 3.790 | .263 | 5 |
| 6 | 1.771 | 7.715 | .129 | .564 | 4.355 | .229 | 6 |
| 7 | 1.948 | 9.487 | .105 | .513 | 4.868 | .205 | 7 |
| 8 | 2.143 | 11.435 | .087 | .466 | 5.334 | .187 | 8 |
| 9 | 2.357 | 13.579 | .073 | .424 | 5.759 | .173 | 9 |
| 10 | 2.593 | 15.937 | .062 | .385 | 6.144 | .162 | 10 |
| 11 | 2.853 | 18.531 | .053 | .350 | 6.495 | .153 | 11 |
| 12 | 3.138 | 21.384 | .046 | .318 | 6.813 | .146 | 12 |
| 13 | 3.452 | 24.522 | .040 | .289 | 7.103 | .140 | 13 |
| 14 | 3.797 | 27.974 | .035 | .263 | 7.366 | .135 | 14 |
| 15 | 4.177 | 31.772 | .031 | .239 | 7.606 | .131 | 15 |
| 16 | 4.594 | 35.949 | .027 | .217 | 7.823 | .127 | 16 |
| 17 | 5.054 | 40.544 | .024 | .197 | 8.021 | .124 | 17 |
| 18 | 5.559 | 45.599 | .021 | .179 | 8.201 | .121 | 18 |
| 19 | 6.115 | 51.159 | .019 | .163 | 8.364 | .119 | 19 |
| 20 | 6.727 | 57.274 | .017 | .148 | 8.513 | .117 | 20 |
| 21 | 7.400 | 64.002 | .015 | .135 | 8.648 | .115 | 21 |
| 22 | 8.140 | 71.402 | .014 | .122 | 8.771 | .114 | 22 |
| 23 | 8.954 | 79.543 | .012 | .111 | 8.883 | .112 | 23 |
| 24 | 9.849 | 88.497 | .011 | .101 | 8.984 | .111 | 24 |
| 25 | 10.834 | 98.347 | .010 | .092 | 9.077 | .110 | 25 |

| | | | | | | | |
|---|---|---|---|---|---|---|---|
| 26 | .109 | 9.160 | .083 | .009 | 109.181 | 11.918 | 26 |
| 27 | .108 | 9.237 | .076 | .008 | 121.099 | 13.109 | 27 |
| 28 | .107 | 9.306 | .069 | .007 | 134.209 | 14.420 | 28 |
| 29 | .106 | 9.369 | .063 | .006 | 148.630 | 15.863 | 29 |
| 30 | .106 | 9.426 | .057 | .006 | 164.494 | 17.449 | 30 |
| 31 | .105 | 9.479 | .052 | .005 | 181.943 | 19.194 | 31 |
| 32 | .104 | 9.526 | .047 | .004 | 201.137 | 21.113 | 32 |
| 33 | .104 | 9.569 | .043 | .004 | 222.251 | 23.225 | 33 |
| 34 | .104 | 9.608 | .039 | .004 | 245.476 | 25.547 | 34 |
| 35 | .103 | 9.644 | .035 | .003 | 271.024 | 28.102 | 35 |
| 36 | .103 | 9.676 | .032 | .003 | 299.126 | 30.912 | 36 |
| 37 | .103 | 9.705 | .029 | .003 | 330.039 | 34.003 | 37 |
| 38 | .102 | 9.732 | .026 | .002 | 364.043 | 37.404 | 38 |
| 39 | .102 | 9.756 | .024 | .002 | 401.447 | 41.144 | 39 |
| 40 | .102 | 9.779 | .022 | .002 | 442.592 | 45.259 | 40 |
| 41 | .102 | 9.799 | .020 | .002 | 487.851 | 49.785 | 41 |
| 42 | .101 | 9.817 | .018 | .001 | 537.636 | 54.763 | 42 |
| 43 | .101 | 9.833 | .016 | .001 | 592.400 | 60.240 | 43 |
| 44 | .101 | 9.849 | .015 | .001 | 652.640 | 66.264 | 44 |
| 45 | .101 | 9.862 | .013 | .001 | 718.904 | 72.890 | 45 |
| 46 | .101 | 9.875 | .012 | .001 | 791.795 | 80.179 | 46 |
| 47 | .101 | 9.886 | .011 | .001 | 871.974 | 88.197 | 47 |
| 48 | .101 | 9.896 | .010 | .001 | 960.172 | 97.017 | 48 |
| 49 | .100 | 9.906 | .009 | .000 | 1057.189 | 106.718 | 49 |
| 50 | .100 | 9.914 | .008 | .000 | 1163.908 | 117.390 | 50 |
| 51 | .100 | 9.922 | .007 | .000 | 1281.299 | 129.129 | 51 |
| 52 | .100 | 9.929 | .007 | .000 | 1410.429 | 142.042 | 52 |
| 53 | .100 | 9.935 | .006 | .000 | 1552.472 | 156.247 | 53 |
| 54 | .100 | 9.941 | .005 | .000 | 1708.719 | 171.871 | 54 |
| 55 | .100 | 9.947 | .005 | .000 | 1880.591 | 189.059 | 55 |
| 56 | .100 | 9.951 | .004 | .000 | 2069.650 | 207.965 | 56 |
| 57 | .100 | 9.956 | .004 | .000 | 2277.615 | 228.761 | 57 |
| 58 | .100 | 9.960 | .003 | .000 | 2506.377 | 251.637 | 58 |
| 59 | .100 | 9.963 | .003 | .000 | 2758.014 | 276.801 | 59 |
| 60 | .100 | 9.967 | .003 | .000 | 3034.816 | 304.481 | 60 |

# Appendix 3: Mathematical Tables at 8%, 10%, 12%, 15% (cont.)

**RATE 12%**

| PERIODS | AMOUNT OF 1 How $1 will grow at compound interest. | AMOUNT OF 1 PER PERIOD How $1 a year will grow. | SINKING FUND Amount per year needed to grow to $1. | PRESENT VALUE OF 1 What $1 payable n years from now is worth. | PRESENT VALUE OF 1 PER PERIOD What $1 payable each year is worth today. | PARTIAL PAYMENT Annuity worth $1 today. |
|---|---|---|---|---|---|---|
| 1 | 1.120 | 1.000 | 1.000 | .892 | .892 | 1.120 |
| 2 | 1.254 | 2.120 | .471 | .797 | 1.690 | .591 |
| 3 | 1.404 | 3.374 | .296 | .711 | 2.401 | .416 |
| 4 | 1.573 | 4.779 | .209 | .635 | 3.037 | .329 |
| 5 | 1.762 | 6.352 | .157 | .567 | 3.604 | .277 |
| 6 | 1.973 | 8.115 | .123 | .506 | 4.111 | .243 |
| 7 | 2.210 | 10.089 | .099 | .452 | 4.563 | .219 |
| 8 | 2.475 | 12.299 | .081 | .403 | 4.967 | .201 |
| 9 | 2.773 | 14.775 | .067 | .360 | 5.328 | .187 |
| 10 | 3.105 | 17.548 | .056 | .321 | 5.650 | .176 |
| 11 | 3.478 | 20.654 | .048 | .287 | 5.937 | .168 |
| 12 | 3.895 | 24.133 | .041 | .256 | 6.194 | .161 |
| 13 | 4.363 | 28.029 | .035 | .229 | 6.423 | .155 |
| 14 | 4.887 | 32.392 | .030 | .204 | 6.628 | .150 |
| 15 | 5.473 | 37.279 | .026 | .182 | 6.810 | .146 |
| 16 | 6.130 | 42.753 | .023 | .163 | 6.973 | .143 |
| 17 | 6.866 | 48.883 | .020 | .145 | 7.119 | .140 |
| 18 | 7.689 | 55.749 | .017 | .130 | 7.249 | .137 |
| 19 | 8.612 | 63.439 | .015 | .116 | 7.365 | .135 |
| 20 | 9.646 | 72.052 | .013 | .103 | 7.469 | .133 |
| 21 | 10.803 | 81.698 | .012 | .092 | 7.562 | .132 |
| 22 | 12.100 | 92.502 | .010 | .082 | 7.644 | .130 |
| 23 | 13.552 | 104.602 | .009 | .073 | 7.718 | .129 |
| 24 | 15.178 | 118.155 | .008 | .065 | 7.784 | .128 |
| 25 | 17.000 | 133.333 | .007 | .058 | 7.843 | .127 |

| | | | | | | | |
|---|---|---|---|---|---|---|---|
| 26 | .126 | 7.895 | .052 | .006 | 150.333 | 19.040 | 26 |
| 27 | .125 | 7.942 | .046 | .005 | 169.374 | 21.324 | 27 |
| 28 | .125 | 7.984 | .041 | .005 | 190.698 | 23.883 | 28 |
| 29 | .124 | 8.021 | .037 | .004 | 214.582 | 26.749 | 29 |
| 30 | .124 | 8.055 | .033 | .004 | 241.332 | 29.959 | 30 |
| 31 | .123 | 8.084 | .029 | .003 | 271.292 | 33.555 | 31 |
| 32 | .123 | 8.111 | .026 | .003 | 304.847 | 37.581 | 32 |
| 33 | .122 | 8.135 | .023 | .002 | 342.429 | 42.091 | 33 |
| 34 | .122 | 8.156 | .021 | .002 | 384.520 | 47.142 | 34 |
| 35 | .122 | 8.175 | .018 | .002 | 431.663 | 52.799 | 35 |
| 36 | .122 | 8.192 | .016 | .002 | 484.463 | 59.135 | 36 |
| 37 | .121 | 8.207 | .015 | .001 | 543.598 | 66.231 | 37 |
| 38 | .121 | 8.220 | .013 | .001 | 609.830 | 74.179 | 38 |
| 39 | .121 | 8.233 | .012 | .001 | 684.010 | 83.081 | 39 |
| 40 | .121 | 8.243 | .010 | .001 | 767.091 | 93.050 | 40 |
| 41 | .121 | 8.253 | .009 | .001 | 860.142 | 104.217 | 41 |
| 42 | .121 | 8.261 | .008 | .001 | 964.359 | 116.723 | 42 |
| 43 | .120 | 8.269 | .007 | .000 | 1081.082 | 130.729 | 43 |
| 44 | .120 | 8.276 | .006 | .000 | 1211.812 | 146.417 | 44 |
| 45 | .120 | 8.282 | .006 | .000 | 1358.230 | 163.987 | 45 |
| 46 | .120 | 8.287 | .005 | .000 | 1522.217 | 183.666 | 46 |
| 47 | .120 | 8.292 | .004 | .000 | 1705.883 | 205.706 | 47 |
| 48 | .120 | 8.297 | .004 | .000 | 1911.589 | 230.390 | 48 |
| 49 | .120 | 8.301 | .003 | .000 | 2141.980 | 258.037 | 49 |
| 50 | .120 | 8.304 | .003 | .000 | 2400.018 | 289.002 | 50 |
| 51 | .120 | 8.307 | .003 | .000 | 2689.020 | 323.682 | 51 |
| 52 | .120 | 8.310 | .002 | .000 | 3012.702 | 362.524 | 52 |
| 53 | .120 | 8.312 | .002 | .000 | 3375.227 | 406.027 | 53 |
| 54 | .120 | 8.315 | .002 | .000 | 3781.254 | 454.750 | 54 |
| 55 | .120 | 8.316 | .001 | .000 | 4236.005 | 509.320 | 55 |
| 56 | .120 | 8.318 | .001 | .000 | 4745.325 | 570.439 | 56 |
| 57 | .120 | 8.320 | .001 | .000 | 5315.764 | 638.891 | 57 |
| 58 | .120 | 8.321 | .001 | .000 | 5954.656 | 715.558 | 58 |
| 59 | .120 | 8.322 | .001 | .000 | 6670.215 | 801.425 | 59 |
| 60 | .120 | 8.324 | .001 | .000 | 7471.641 | 897.596 | 60 |

# Appendix 3: Mathematical Tables at 8%, 10%, 12%, 15% (cont.)

| PERIODS | AMOUNT OF 1 How $1 will grow at compound interest. | AMOUNT OF 1 PER PERIOD How $1 a year will grow. | SINKING FUND Amount per year needed to grow to $1. | PRESENT VALUE OF 1 What $1 payable n years from now is worth. | PRESENT VALUE OF 1 PER PERIOD What $1 payable each year is worth today. | PARTIAL PAYMENT Annuity worth $1 today. | PERIODS |
|---|---|---|---|---|---|---|---|
| **RATE 15%** | | | | | | | |
| 1 | 1.150 | 1.000 | 1.000 | .869 | .869 | 1.150 | 1 |
| 2 | 1.322 | 2.150 | .465 | .756 | 1.625 | .615 | 2 |
| 3 | 1.520 | 3.472 | .287 | .657 | 2.283 | .437 | 3 |
| 4 | 1.749 | 4.993 | .200 | .571 | 2.854 | .350 | 4 |
| 5 | 2.011 | 6.742 | .148 | .497 | 3.352 | .298 | 5 |
| 6 | 2.313 | 8.753 | .114 | .432 | 3.784 | .264 | 6 |
| 7 | 2.660 | 11.066 | .090 | .375 | 4.160 | .240 | 7 |
| 8 | 3.059 | 13.726 | .072 | .326 | 4.487 | .222 | 8 |
| 9 | 3.517 | 16.785 | .059 | .284 | 4.771 | .209 | 9 |
| 10 | 4.045 | 20.303 | .049 | .247 | 5.018 | .199 | 10 |
| 11 | 4.652 | 24.349 | .041 | .214 | 5.233 | .191 | 11 |
| 12 | 5.350 | 29.001 | .034 | .186 | 5.420 | .184 | 12 |
| 13 | 6.152 | 34.351 | .029 | .162 | 5.583 | .179 | 13 |
| 14 | 7.075 | 40.504 | .024 | .141 | 5.724 | .174 | 14 |
| 15 | 8.137 | 47.580 | .021 | .122 | 5.847 | .171 | 15 |
| 16 | 9.357 | 55.717 | .017 | .106 | 5.954 | .167 | 16 |
| 17 | 10.761 | 65.075 | .015 | .092 | 6.047 | .165 | 17 |
| 18 | 12.375 | 75.836 | .013 | .080 | 6.127 | .163 | 18 |
| 19 | 14.231 | 88.211 | .011 | .070 | 6.198 | .161 | 19 |
| 20 | 16.366 | 102.443 | .009 | .061 | 6.259 | .159 | 20 |
| 21 | 18.821 | 118.810 | .008 | .053 | 6.312 | .158 | 21 |
| 22 | 21.644 | 137.631 | .007 | .046 | 6.358 | .157 | 22 |
| 23 | 24.891 | 159.276 | .006 | .040 | 6.398 | .156 | 23 |
| 24 | 28.625 | 184.167 | .005 | .034 | 6.433 | .155 | 24 |
| 25 | 32.918 | 212.793 | .004 | .030 | 6.464 | .154 | 25 |

| | | | | | | | |
|---|---|---|---|---|---|---|---|
| 26 | .154 | 6.490 | .026 | .004 | 245.711 | 37.856 | 26 |
| 27 | .153 | 6.513 | .022 | .003 | 283.568 | 43.535 | 27 |
| 28 | .153 | 6.533 | .019 | .003 | 327.104 | 50.065 | 28 |
| 29 | .152 | 6.550 | .017 | .002 | 377.169 | 57.575 | 29 |
| 30 | .152 | 6.565 | .015 | .002 | 434.745 | 66.211 | 30 |
| 31 | .151 | 6.579 | .013 | .001 | 500.956 | 76.143 | 31 |
| 32 | .151 | 6.590 | .011 | .001 | 577.100 | 87.565 | 32 |
| 33 | .151 | 6.600 | .009 | .001 | 664.665 | 100.699 | 33 |
| 34 | .151 | 6.609 | .008 | .001 | 765.365 | 115.804 | 34 |
| 35 | .151 | 6.616 | .007 | .001 | 881.170 | 133.175 | 35 |
| 36 | .150 | 6.623 | .006 | .000 | 1014.345 | 153.151 | 36 |
| 37 | .150 | 6.628 | .005 | .000 | 1167.497 | 176.124 | 37 |
| 38 | .150 | 6.633 | .004 | .000 | 1343.622 | 202.543 | 38 |
| 39 | .150 | 6.638 | .004 | .000 | 1546.165 | 232.924 | 39 |
| 40 | .150 | 6.641 | .003 | .000 | 1779.090 | 267.863 | 40 |
| 41 | .150 | 6.645 | .003 | .000 | 2046.953 | 308.043 | 41 |
| 42 | .150 | 6.647 | .002 | .000 | 2354.996 | 354.249 | 42 |
| 43 | .150 | 6.650 | .002 | .000 | 2709.246 | 407.386 | 43 |
| 44 | .150 | 6.652 | .002 | .000 | 3116.633 | 468.495 | 44 |
| 45 | .150 | 6.654 | .001 | .000 | 3585.128 | 538.769 | 45 |
| 46 | .150 | 6.655 | .001 | .000 | 4123.897 | 619.584 | 46 |
| 47 | .150 | 6.657 | .001 | .000 | 4743.482 | 712.522 | 47 |
| 48 | .150 | 6.658 | .001 | .000 | 5456.004 | 819.400 | 48 |
| 49 | .150 | 6.659 | .001 | .000 | 6275.405 | 942.310 | 49 |
| 50 | .150 | 6.660 | .000 | .000 | 7217.716 | 1083.657 | 50 |
| 51 | .150 | 6.661 | .000 | .000 | 8301.373 | 1246.206 | 51 |
| 52 | .150 | 6.662 | .000 | .000 | 9547.579 | 1433.136 | 52 |
| 53 | .150 | 6.662 | .000 | .000 | 10980.716 | 1648.107 | 53 |
| 54 | .150 | 6.663 | .000 | .000 | 12628.824 | 1895.323 | 54 |
| 55 | .150 | 6.663 | .000 | .000 | 14524.147 | 2179.622 | 55 |
| 56 | .150 | 6.664 | .000 | .000 | 16703.770 | 2506.565 | 56 |
| 57 | .150 | 6.664 | .000 | .000 | 19210.335 | 2882.550 | 57 |
| 58 | .150 | 6.664 | .000 | .000 | 22092.885 | 3314.932 | 58 |
| 59 | .150 | 6.664 | .000 | .000 | 25407.818 | 3812.172 | 59 |
| 60 | .150 | 6.665 | .000 | .000 | 29219.991 | 4383.998 | 60 |

# Appendix 4: Term Insurance Prices per $1,000

| AGE | Reducing | | Yearly renewable | | | | 5-year, non-par | |
|---|---|---|---|---|---|---|---|---|
| | 1960 | 1980 | Occidental 1980 | Ontario Med. (1980) (less 50%) | Occidental 1960 | Occidental 1980 | Dominion 1981 | Great West 1980 |
| 20 | 3.51 | | 1.50 | | 3.91 | | | |
| 21 | | | | | | | | |
| 22 | | | | | | | | |
| 23 | | | | | | | | |
| 24 | | | | | | | | |
| 25 | 3.65 | 1.60 | 1.55 | | 4.07 | 2.18 | 1.95 | 1.93 |
| 26 | | | | | | | | |
| 27 | | | | | | | | |
| 28 | | | | | | | | |
| 29 | | | | | | | | |
| 30 | 3.90 | | 1.67 | 1.00 | 4.39 | | | |
| 31 | | | | | | | | |
| 32 | | | | | | | | |
| 33 | | | | | | | | |
| 34 | | | | | | | | |
| 35 | 4.36 | 3.03 | 2.23 | 1.27 | 5.06 | 2.65 | 2.46 | 2.35 |
| 36 | | | | | | | | |
| 37 | | | | | | | | |

| | | | | | | | |
|---|---|---|---|---|---|---|---|
| 38 | | | | | | | |
| 39 | | | | | | | |
| 40 | 5.48 | 3.06 | 1.93 | 6.50 | | | |
| 41 | | | | | | | |
| 42 | | | | | | | |
| 43 | | | | | | | |
| 44 | | | | | | | |
| 45 | 7.37 | 4.60 | 4.99 | 9.02 | 5.58 | 5.09 | 4.68 |
| 46 | | | | | | | |
| 47 | 7.25 | | | | | | |
| 48 | | | | | | | |
| 49 | | | | | | | |
| 50 | 10.36 | 7.24 | 7.60 | | | | |
| 51 | | | | | | | |
| 52 | | | | | | | |
| 53 | | | | | | | |
| 54 | | | | | | | |
| 55 | 15.64 | 11.46 | 12.43 | | 13.20 | 11.62 | 10.11 |
| 56 | | | | | | | |
| 57 | | | | | | | |
| 58 | | | | | | | |
| 59 | | | | | | | |
| 60 | | | | | | | |
| Minimum amount (in thousands) | 5 | 250 | 80 | 100 | 100 | 100 | 100 |

# Appendix 5: Mortality and Life-Expectancy Tables

| | NUMBER DYING PER 1,000 | | | | | | Life expectancy: How many years the average person your age will live | |
|---|---|---|---|---|---|---|---|---|
| | American Experience | U.S. Life | American | Statistics Canada | | | | |
| Your Age | 1843-58 | 1910 | Men Ultimate | 1943 | 1954 | 1982* | Age | Years |
| 20 | 7.23 | 4.68 | 3.92 | 2.41 | | ⎫ 1.4 | 20 | 52 |
| 25 | 7.18 | 5.54 | 4.31 | 2.57 | .89 | ⎬ 1.4 | 25 | 47 |
| 30 | 7.20 | 6.51 | 4.46 | 2.60 | 1.00 / 1.08 | ⎬ 1.3 | 30 | 43 |
| 35 | 7.32 | 8.04 | 4.78 | 3.18 | 1.41 | ⎬ 1.6 | 35 | 38 |
| 40 | 7.65 | 9.39 | 5.84 | 4.29 | 2.36 | ⎭ 2.6 | 40 | 33 |

| | | | | | | | | |
|---|---|---|---|---|---|---|---|---|
| 45 | 8.28 | 11.52 | 7.94 | 6.00 | 4.02 | } 4.3 | 45 | 29 |
| 50 | 9.62 | 14.37 | 11.58 | 8.99 | 6.72 | } 7.5 | 50 | 25 |
| 55 | 11.99 | 20.03 | 17.47 | 13.55 | 10.91 | } 12.4 | 55 | 21 |
| 60 | 15.46 | 28.58 | 26.68 | 20.50 | 17.57 | } 19.2 | 60 | 17 |
| 65 | 19.80 | 41.06 | 40.66 | 31.38 | 27.61 | } 30.6 | 65 | 14 |
| 70 | 23.21 | 59.52 | 61.47 | 48.75 | 39.66 | | 70 | 11 |

*Statistics Canada now gives 5-year average mortality, rather than individual ages.

# Appendix 6: Table of Commuted Values

*COMMUTATION RATE 3%*

| Number of years to end of period | Commuted value of $10 a month | Number of years to end of period | Commuted value of $10 a month |
|---|---|---|---|
| 25 | $2123 | 14 | $1377 |
| 24 | 2065 | 13 | 1297 |
| 23 | 2005 | 12 | 1214 |
| 22 | 1943 | 11 | 1128 |
| 21 | 1880 | 10 | 1040 |
| 20 | 1814 | 9 | 949 |
| 19 | 1747 | 8 | 856 |
| 18 | 1677 | 7 | 760 |
| 17 | 1605 | 6 | 661 |
| 16 | 1532 | 5 | 558 |
| 15 | 1456 | 4 to 1 | 453 |

# Appendix 7: Section of Transcript of Libel Trial

(With commentary by J. J. Brown)

LAWYER: "I am trying to get at the question of authorship..."

GUTWILLIG: "Gorman handed me the manuscript. I made slight changes."

(At this moment Gorman looked as if he had an uncontrollable internal fire. He turned deep red, shuffled in his seat, and sneaked a look at the judge.)

LAWYER: "What changes did you make?"

GUTWILLIG: "I changed a few initials."

LAWYER: "What initials did you change?"

(Objection from opposing counsel. The judge reserved judgment on the point.)

LAWYER: "What did you change? Was J. J. Brown mentioned?"

(Again counsel objected, and the judge reserved.)

LAWYER: "What name did you take out of the article?" (The same ritual of objection and reserve.)

GUTWILLIG (looking pale and very scared) TO THE JUDGE: "Do I answer?"

JUSTICE HANNON (in a terrible voice): "Answer!"

GUTWILLIG: "J. J. Brown."

(There ensued a long silence. Even the judge had nothing to say.)

# Index